Gabriel Gaté is Australia's favourite French accent, loved for his delicious recipes and sound advice. A popular presence on television and radio and in magazines and author of nineteen cookbooks, he brought us bestsellers such as *Good Food for Men* and *Weekend on a Plate*. In 2002 Gaté confirmed his role as one of the country's best educators about good eating with the release of the popular *How to Teach Kids to Cook*.

GABRIEL GATÉ
guide to everyday cooking

PHOTOGRAPHY BY ADRIAN LANDER

A SUE HINES BOOK
ALLEN & UNWIN

First published in 2003

A Sue Hines Book
Allen & Unwin
83 Alexander Street
Crows Nest NSW 2065
Australia
Phone: (61 2) 8425 0100
Fax: (61 2) 9906 2218
Email: info@allenandunwin.com
Web: www.allenandunwin.com

National Library of Australia
Cataloguing-in-Publication entry:

Gaté, Gabriel, 1955–.
    Guide to everyday cooking.
    ISBN 1 74114 033 1.
    1. Cookery. I. Lander, Adrian. II. Title.
    641.5

Grateful thanks to Country Road, Minimax
and Supply and Demand.

Typeset by Pauline Haas
Designed by MAU Design
Printed in Hong Kong through Colorcraft

CONTENTS

make

mess

shop

Oranges
Garlic
Flour
Chicken
Milk
Eggs
Pasta

INTRODUCTION

It's possible for almost anyone to be a good, happy everyday cook. You may have had the chance to learn at a young age from your mother, father or grandparents. You can take cooking classes and practise what you have been taught, or you can teach yourself with a little help from others. Over the years, after teaching cooking to people of all ages and writing cookbooks to help readers become better cooks, I have worked out a way to stimulate, inspire and help home cooks teach themselves. The secret is to learn to cook new dishes regularly in order to become familiar with new ingredients, new tastes, new textures and new techniques.

Start with simple preparations and you'll be encouraged by your quick progress. Practise dishes you love eating yourself. Be kind to yourself, accepting gracefully the dishes that turn out less than perfect. And most importantly, don't give up after the first try. Home cooking needs to be varied, both for pleasure and good health. In this guide, you'll find 200 recipes and plenty of information on how to teach yourself, on health issues, shopping and equipment. Take time to cook. Most everyday meals take 20 to 45 minutes to prepare. At the weekend or whenever you have a little more time, cook those hearty casseroles that are easy to make but take a bit longer. Remember that the little effort required at the beginning is rewarded many times over by the great life skills you learn. And the joys are priceless.

Teach Yourself to Cook

I have learned and been inspired about food and cooking by many people and I am very grateful to them. However, if I am a competent cook now, it is because I have taught myself to cook. To teach yourself to cook you must make time, be curious and cook regularly. It's not as difficult as you may think. Each time you cook, you'll become a better cook.

A new dish learned every month means you can cook sixty different dishes after five years. Anyone able to cook sixty different dishes is a good cook.

How to Become a Creative Cook

- Increase your repertoire by learning to cook a new dish once a month. Watch cookery shows on TV, paying attention to techniques with which you may be unfamiliar, such as chopping or carving.

- Read the recipe for a new dish carefully before doing the shopping. Try to visualise the various steps and the finished dish.

- Remember, a recipe is only a guide. However, if you do wish to follow the recipe closely, concentrate during the cooking.

- Allow yourself plenty of time when you first cook a new dish.

- Practise a new dish three times within a month so as to memorise the steps and master the difficulties, and then go on to adapt it to your taste.

- Don't try a new dish for the first time when cooking for an important occasion. Practise it first to minimise stress.

- Learn a simple dish first, then create your own variation of it. For example, learn to grill a fish fillet, then next time, grill a fish fillet which has been marinated in olive oil, chilli and coriander, and serve it with a mashed potato mixed with chopped olives.

- Learn new cutting techniques, such as julienne (long thin sticks).

- Learn to cook dishes from different countries, such as France, Italy, India or China to increase your knowledge of ingredients. Travel overseas and before you go, read about the cuisine of the place you will visit (the Lonely Planet publications are excellent).

- Familiarise yourself with one new spice and one new herb each month.

- Taste foods you have never tried before in order to increase your memory of flavours.

- Buy a cut of meat you have never tried before. And, next time you buy fish, try something different.
- Try to remember which seasoning goes well with which food, for example, lemon with fish, basil with pasta.
- Use your sense of smell when you buy food – sniff the peaches, melons, herbs and cheeses.
- Get to know which foods are in season, for example, cherries appear in spring, apples are best in autumn.
- Question your butcher, fishmonger, greengrocer and other shopkeepers about food preparation and cooking.
- Visit a market or the closest good food store regularly.
- Keep staple foods, such as pasta, rice, flour, oil and spices on hand in the pantry so you can whip up simple dishes at a moment's notice.
- Include new cookware and electrical appliances on your Christmas and birthday wish list.
- Join a cookery course at least once in your life so you can learn new techniques.

Treasure Your Cooking Heritage

Our parents give us an identity, and their food is part of that. Treasure it.

- Learn to cook your favourites among the dishes that your parents (or grandparents) make. Record as much information as possible about the way your relatives choose, prepare and cook food. Write recipes down, key them into your computer or video the process. In particular, record your family's festive family dishes.
- Continue family traditions, such as making scones or Christmas pudding, baking Anzac biscuits, colouring Easter eggs, bottling tomato sauce, making fresh pasta and favourite family cakes.
- If you are have recently migrated to Australia, continue to cook some of the foods from your homeland and show your children and friends how to prepare them.
- If you are a new arrival, learn to cook the dishes popular in your new country.

Kids and Cooking

As a parent I feel it is important to share my cooking knowledge with my children so as to establish a positive image of cooking and give them some basic understanding about food preparation. This is essential for their own independence and to help them see the link between good food and good health. It goes without saying that this applies to boys as well as girls.

Involve children young: little children as young as two or three years of age are fascinated by the preparation of food. They know that Mum or Dad is cooking something yummy and they want to take part in the fun. For them, cooking is a game of colour, texture, shape and taste. It pays to be a very patient and tolerant parent and to let children participate in many small tasks, such as shelling peas, measuring rice, turning on the tap to fill a saucepan with water for cooking pasta, and so on. Remember to be positive and encouraging always. Each time they help they can learn a new skill and, as they grow older, they will become happy, skilful cooks.

Many parents make the mistake of waiting too long before asking children to contribute to food preparation. The best time to teach kids to cook at home is during primary school and early secondary school. At that age children can safely cook many dishes, such as noodles, pasta, rice, soup, sauces, dressings, casseroles, salads, desserts and cakes. Once they are teenagers, if they have never taken part in the cooking, it will be much harder for them to start as they are not in the habit. In addition, they tend to have a busy lifestyle with school and social activities. Fortunately, some schools successfully teach cooking to teenagers.

Grandparents can play an important role. My grandmother taught me many little things in the kitchen. She was a talented cook and loving grandparent, and I am forever grateful to her.

Take your kids shopping as much of the skill in preparing food lies in learning to buy and recognise fresh food. Take small children shopping and play games with them, such as 'Can you put six unblemished apples in this bag for me?' Ask them to find things at the supermarket, such as spaghetti, rice or olive oil. Teach them to choose ripe fruit. Teach them the names of herbs, fish and cuts of meat. Help them recognise quality by smell, for example in a mango, peach or pineapple or a bunch of mint or basil.

Give children specific kitchen tasks from an early age, such as setting the table, washing or drying dishes, putting vegetable and fruit scraps in the compost bin and taking out the rubbish. Children should learn these skills, and they are best learnt as part of a daily routine.

Health and Safety

All the best cooks I have met are interested in the well-being of those they cook for, and talking about health is an important part of an everyday cookbook. Parents want their children to be healthy. People have different ideas about what good health means, but there are general healthy-eating principles that apply to us all. The most important is to consume a wide variety of foods. This means a cook must learn to cook many different dishes, using many different ingredients. The food has more goodness when it's fresh, when it's not overcooked and when it's prepared following some basic rules of hygiene. You will find guidelines throughout this book that will help you with health issues. See the hints on how to keep your weight down on page 64, how to take care of your heart on page 101 and how to look after yourself if you have diabetes on page 51.

Cooking and Eating for Well-being and a Longer Life

- Eat a wide variety from all the food groups – vegetables, cereals, fruits, fish and meat and dairy products.
- Find out which foods make you feel good and happy, and which ones don't suit you, for instance, if you have a particular problem such as high blood pressure, bad digestion, etc.
- Eat meals at regular times and don't miss meals.
- Eat in a relaxed atmosphere; sit down and take your time.
- Enjoy a copious breakfast for lasting energy.
- Enjoy a nourishing lunch – not too little, not too much.
- At dinnertime, eat just enough to satisfy your appetite, and eat at least three hours before going to bed.
- Learn to cook using a minimum of fat, salt and sugar (except for special occasions).
- Avoid fatty, salty and very sweet foods as snacks.
- Drink plenty of water. Drink alcohol and fizzy, sweet drinks in moderation.
- Learn to use herbs and spices as seasonings. Use hot, spicy seasonings in moderation.
- Keep fit and exercise daily. Enjoy life and don't work too hard.

Good Teeth Mean Happy Eating

The management of oral health is most important for the enjoyment and ease of eating, chewing, digesting, speaking ... and smiling! A regular checkup at the dentist is a must.

Dentists advise us to brush our teeth, using fluoride toothpaste, twice a day – once after breakfast then again after the evening meal. They also highly recommend flossing daily, preferably in the evening after brushing the teeth. Only floss can remove the build up of food between the teeth.

Another important way to keep our teeth and gums in good nick is to adopt a balanced diet and eat a wide variety from all the food groups, especially foods rich in calcium, such as low-fat milk, cheese and other dairy products, as well as foods rich in vitamin C, such as vegetables and fruits.

Tooth decay is the result of the action in the mouth of bacteria, with sugar being transformed into acid. It is this acid that decays teeth. The best way to avoid this decay is to manage your consumption of sugar:

Avoid adding sugar to foods like cereals, fruits and sauces. If you do add sugar to tea and coffee, try cutting down gradually. For example, if you take two teaspoons of sugar in your coffee, cut it down to one and three-quarter teaspoons for two weeks, then reduce it to one and a half teaspoons for another two weeks, and so on. I used this technique successfully myself a few years ago and you really don't notice it much. Of course, it helps not to keep sugar on the table.

Avoid sweet snacks – instead of chocolate bars, muesli bars, sugar-coated nuts and lollies, eat fruit, nuts, raw vegetables, freshly squeezed juices or even a glass of water. (Note that dried fruits are very sweet.) It is better to eat sweets at the end of a savoury meal rather than between meals, and experts recommend keeping our sugar attacks down to three per day.

Avoid sweet drinks. In terms of oral health, the best drink is water from the tap. Milk and freshly squeezed fruit and vegetable juices are preferable to sweetened drinks, like fizzy soft drinks and cordials.

Ask for sugar-free medicine as many medications are sweetened or have a sugar coating. If you take a lot of medication or pills, ask for a sugar-free from.

Babies and children

Informative brochures on the oral health of babies are published by various health organisations and are freely available from dentists, pharmacists and community health centres. From one such brochure, published by the NSW Health Department (Australia), I learned something I never knew when my own children were babies: 'Babies are not born with decay-causing bacteria (germs). It is passed to them from others, especially parents . . . Really good cleaning of your own teeth and gums every day will help keep your baby's teeth healthy.' But please don't stop kissing your baby!

When a baby's teeth come through, parents are advised to clean them using a small brush (toothpaste is unnecessary for infants) or wipe them at least once a day with a clean face washer or cotton gauze. Parents should also begin flossing their children's teeth as soon as possible. This is an interesting challenge! Inspect your child's mouth regularly to check for any problems, and visit the dentist with your baby soon after the first birthday. It is not unusual for toddlers to have tooth decay, and to prevent decay, refrain from putting sweet drinks, such as juice, cordial or soft drinks in your baby's bottle. Only four types of fluid are acceptable in babies' bottles: mother's milk, infant formula, cow's milk or soy milk, and water.

Keeping Your Hands in Good Shape

In the preparation of food, apart from our brain and our eyes, we use our hands more than any other tool. They allow us to have very precise control over the food and equipment we use, and the sensitivity of the hands is an important part of the joy of cooking. It is fun and very satisfying to neatly peel an apple, slice a mushroom, decorate a fruit tart or ice a cake.

When cooking, make sure your nails and hands are clean. Always wash your hands with soap and dry them well before touching food, then wash them again when you change from one type of food to another, for example, when changing from preparing meat to vegetables, or from fish to desserts.

Cover injuries, cuts and burns when cooking. Wear an appropriate waterproof dressings, and note that there are some cases where it is best not to handle food, so if you have an infection, consider seeing the doctor.

When you cut yourself the first step is to stop or manage the bleeding. Cover the cut with an appropriate dressing or piece of clean cloth several layers thick, avoiding tissue or paper that will disintegrate and disturb the wound. When you wrap the cut, try to ensure that the edges of the wound are not gaping. This will help it heal rapidly. If the cut is serious and requires medical attention, see the doctor or go to the hospital. If medical help is not available, clean the wound with a diluted antiseptic or clean water, once the bleeding has stopped. Don't disturb any forming clots as they are part of the healing process.

A **burn** is caused by dry heat, electricity, sun or excess friction. A **scald** is caused by moist heat, such as water, steam or oil. Treat any burns immediately, whether serious or not, by immersion in cold water, or cover them with a wet cloth for 10–20 minutes. If the injury is serious, seek medical treatment. If the burn is underneath clothing, remove the clothing provided it comes off easily. If the clothing is stuck to the skin you may risk removing skin as well, and so leave it on and seek medical help.

Do not pierce or break blisters. Cover burns with a clean or sterile, non-stick dressing, or bandage the burnt area very lightly. Rest comfortably and raise the injured hand or limb. Sit up if your face is burnt. Sip water to replace fluids and avoid alcohol.

Safety in the Kitchen

- Keep an eye on oil when deep-frying. If it boils over it may catch fire.
- Don't let children handle hot oil or hot caramel.
- Keep a fire blanket and fire extinguisher near the exit of your kitchen.
- Don't put out an electric fire or burning oil with water. Smother it instead, and if you feel the situation is out of control, call the fire brigade immediately.
- Keep saucepan handles out of the reach of small children.
- Don't leave a hot roasting tray or pan on the bench or stove without warning everybody present.
- Carefully protect your hands with oven mitts or a thick tea towel when handling hot dishes from the oven or stove.
- Don't leave tea towels near or hanging over the stove as they catch fire easily.
- Be cautious when peeling off plastic from microwaved food – the escaping steam can burn you.

Shopping

After I have done my shopping and bought good quality ingredients, I know the dish I want to prepare will be delicious, as long as I concentrate during the cooking. Freshness is all-important to the cook. Those who find cooking difficult (or as they say, hate cooking) often neglect the shopping, take too many shortcuts, buy without choosing, buy too long in advance or cook too long in advance of eating the food, and use too many frozen or precooked foods.

While the beauty and quality of fresh food is stimulating for the cook, food that is past its best discourages the cook. Try to see doing the shopping as part of your social life. Get to know the people you buy from – you may see them twice a week.

The Supermarket

More than three-quarters of all shoppers do most of their supermarket shopping at the store closest to home. All supermarkets are not the same, with the variety available depending greatly on size and the supermarket chain. Personally, I prefer medium-sized supermarkets; not too small, so I can have a reasonable choice, and not too large, so that I can whip round the aisles and do a large shop in twenty minutes. I certainly don't mind driving a few extra minutes to ensure that my needs are satisfied.

In my work as a food writer and presenter, I visit supermarkets several times a week. I find it quite inspiring to discover new ingredients or to renew contact with foods I have not used for a while. There are so many foods available these days and so many I have not tried. Overall, the standard of supermarkets has improved. They offer better breads, cheeses, deli items and a wider variety of cuts of meat and poultry. Free-range eggs are available. The greatest weakness is often the fish section, where you find that almost everything has been frozen and is thawing out – poorly! The ripeness of the fruit also leaves a lot to be desired. I have not seen a good supermarket apricot, plum or peach for a long time. At the same time, the selection of vegetables and herbs has certainly improved.

A Good Greengrocer

- Promotes seasonal food.
- Sells ripe fruit ready to eat, as well as fruit that will be ready in the next few days.
- Is happy to help you select fruit and vegetables.
- Sells a variety of fresh herbs all year round.
- Provides printed information on a range of vegetables, fruits and herbs.
- Will give you ideas on how to prepare unusual fruits, vegetables and herbs, and how to store what you buy.
- Smiles a lot (in contrast to whingeing a lot!)
- Will order special foods for you, such as a specific variety of potatoes or apples.
- Will help you carry, if you wish, your goods to the car or will organise delivery to your home.
- Provides different varieties of the same fruit or vegetable, for example, Granny Smith, Golden Delicious and Royal Gala apples, and both green and white asparagus.
- Sells at least four varieties of potato.
- Gives you a taste of a fruit if you ask.
- Removes damaged fruit and vegetables from the display.

Shopping for Fruit and Vegetables

- Buy the least perishable vegetables, such as potatoes, carrots and pumpkin first then lastly pick up the more delicate greens (e.g. rocket) and fruit (e.g. peaches and raspberries).
- For better flavour and good nutrition, buy fruit and vegetables when they are in season – peaches in summer, apples in autumn, asparagus in spring, cabbage in winter.
- To add spice to your life, make a habit of buying fruit, vegetables and herbs that you have not tried before.
- Plan ahead to provide a variety of vegetables to those you cook for.
- To keep food fresh on hot days, park your car in the shade.
- Learn to touch fruit such as peaches, plums, avocadoes, and melons delicately to gauge their ripeness.
- To assess ripeness and sweetness, smell fruit like pears, apples, pineapples, mangoes, peaches and melons.
- Smell herbs to gauge their quality and to inspire you to cook with them.
- Ask for advice and printed information on preparing vegetables and fruits that are new to you.
- Store potatoes, onions, garlic and uncut pumpkin in a dry place (not in the fridge).
- Most vegetables, for example, carrots, cut pumpkin, zucchini, eggplant, capsicum and broccoli, are best stored in the vegetable crisper of the refrigerator.
- Keep mushrooms in paper bags in the fridge.
- Store apples, pears, bananas, lemons, and oranges in a large fruit bowl in a well-ventilated, cool part of the kitchen and away from the sun.
- Buy fresh vegetables often and consume them soon after purchase. Avoid storing them for more than 3–4 days.
- Store all berries in the refrigerator.
- Store unripe avocadoes in the fruit bowl. Ripe ones can be refrigerated.
- Store fresh herbs in the refrigerator in a sealed freezer bag. They keep well for 4–6 days.

A Good Butcher

- Offers friendly service and advises you on which cut is best for the dish you want to cook.
- Displays printed information about preparing and cooking meat.
- Gives you the meat you select even if you choose a slice in the middle of the tray.
- Offers a wide variety of cuts of meat.
- Does not pile meat too high on the trays.
- Keeps a very clean shop.
- Carefully wraps your meat for transportation home.
- Displays cuts of meat well trimmed of fat and gristle.
- Prepares meat the way you need it, e.g. minces meat to order, cuts meat for a stir-fry, ties a piece of roast with string, etc.
- Displays steak, cutlets and chops that have been sliced to an even thickness.
- Provides some beef cuts that have been aged. The process tenderises meat and gives it more flavour.

Shopping for Meat

- A good cut of beef is a rich, deep red colour – not too dark, not too light.
- Meat is best trimmed of fat and gristle and of any unnecessary bones, and it should have a firm texture.
- Young beef and lamb is paler in colour than older beef and lamb.
- Learn from your butcher by asking questions.
- Buy steak that is evenly sliced.
- Spring is the best time to buy lamb.
- In winter and at the end of a dry summer, beef can be a bit tough.
- The most tender but also more expensive cuts of beef are best served as steak, e.g. porterhouse, scotch fillet and rump.
- The cuts that have a good balance of tenderness and flavour, such as rib roast, sirloin (porterhouse) and rump, are great for roasting.
- Cuts sold as gravy beef, shin, blade and osso bucco, are very tasty but not so tender and need longer cooking. They are best used in dishes such as stews, curries and casseroles.
- Asian butchers generally tend to have a larger selection of pork.

Fresh is Best

Nothing is more important to achieving an excellent dish than the freshness of the ingredients.

Fresh food looks better, smells better and tastes better, and is best for your health.

The older the food, the more nutritional value has disappeared.

Ask shopkeepers to help you recognise freshness.

Fresh ingredients are usually firm in texture. Older foods (particularly vegetables and fish) become limp as they lose moisture.

Shop for fresh fruit and vegetables at least three times a week.

Shop for fish or seafood on the day or the day before you cook it or consume it.

Sliced meat or meat for roasting is best cooked and eaten within 1–3 days of purchase. Minced meat or very thinly sliced meat is best cooked and eaten within 24 hours of purchase.

Poultry is best cooked and eaten within 48 hours of purchase. Minced poultry is best eaten within 24 hours of purchase.

A Good Fishmonger

- Offers a wide variety of fresh whole fish, fish fillets and cutlets at varying prices.
- Keeps the fish shop very clean – it can smell of fish or seafood but it shouldn't be offputting or smell strongly of bleach.
- Sells more fresh fish than frozen fish.
- Keeps the fish on ice or in a very cool atmosphere.
- Displays printed information on preparing and cooking fish and seafood.
- Will advise on which fish may suit the dish you are preparing and what quantity you need.
- Will prepare (scale, gut, cut fins off, fillet) a fish at your request.
- Takes special orders.
- Carefully wraps your fish and seafood for transportation to your home.
- Has a wide variety of fresh, unfrozen seafood, e.g. crab, mussels, prawns, etc.
- Tells you if a fish has been frozen.
- Does not leave fish fillets swimming in trays of water.
- Labels the real name of the fish and its price per kilogram.

Shopping for Fish and Seafood

- Have a good look at the display to gauge what looks fresh.

- Over time, learn to recognise the different varieties of fish and try new ones.

- When a fish is available either whole or in fillets, ask for the whole fish and get the fishmonger to fillet it for you. That way, you'll enjoy a fresher piece of fish.

- Be very specific about the piece of fish you wish to purchase, for example, 'I want that thick piece of flathead fillet on the left of the tray.'

- Get to know the fishmongers by their first name and let them know your name.

- Ask for recommendations, explaining to the fishmonger what you intend to do with the fish, e.g. barbecue, bake, stew, steam, serve to the kids.

- Ask your fishmonger to clean a whole fish for you or to explain how to do it.

- A whole fresh fish has slippery, shiny scales that hold together closely. The eyes are clear and bulging and the flesh appears firm and holds together well.

- Understand that not all varieties of fish are available all the time. The weather, season and where you live determine what is on offer on a particular day.

Equipment

It is a good idea at first to borrow equipment that you use only occasionally.

I value my kitchen tools and equipment highly. Whether it be my knives or my pots and pans, they help me cook more comfortably and with the least effort. Rather than follow trends, buy the tools you need for what they can do for you and the time they will save you. My advice never changes in this regard: buy the best quality you can afford. Beware of very cheap cookware – you will get what you pay for. The average home cook prepares 20,000 meals in a lifetime, and the investment in quality is very well spent. When you shop for equipment, visit a specialised store or large department store, and before you purchase, seek advice from a senior shop assistant, specifying exactly what you will use the equipment for. Remember, cookware is usually on special after Christmas or at the end of the tax year.

Knives

There are few kitchen utensils more precious to a cook than sharp knives. I believe in buying the best knives I can possibly afford, and particularly recommend the so-called 'chef's knives'. Three knives that will do most cutting jobs are:

A **small paring knife** with a straight blade is used to peel fruit, trim vegetables and do many other small jobs.

A **cook's knife** (chef's knife) with a blade about 20 cm (8 in) long, or longer if you can handle it comfortably, is used to cut up most vegetables, especially hard ones, such as carrots and pumpkin. It can also do many other jobs, like cutting pastry into shape and chopping herbs or other ingredients.

A **boning knife**, also called a butcher's knife, with a fairly narrow but rigid blade 15 cm (6 in) long is used to trim fat from meat, slice meat and joint chicken and fish.

I also find one or two other knives useful:

A **Chinese chopper** is great for cutting vegetables and meat when you cook Asian food. Join a Chinese cooking class and learn how to use it well.

A **serrated knife** is useful for slicing bread, tomatoes and some fruits such as pineapple, as well as many other foods.

A **filleting knife** is great for those who love fishing and cooking their catch. A filletting knife has a long, thin, strong, flexible blade with a very pointy tip and is perfect for separating fish fillets from the bones and for finely slicing fish fillets.

A **palette knife**, also called a spatula, is not used for cutting, but is ideal for spreading (as when icing cakes) and for lifting foods such as fish from a frying pan.

Other Useful Cutting Tools

Scissors are necessary for opening food packaging, cutting string and baking paper and so on. Poultry and fish scissors are also very handy for portioning poultry and trimming fish fins and tails. If you have kids, your kitchen scissors will probably often disappear from the knife block!

Peelers for peeling fruits and vegetables. We all need a few as they are sometimes thrown out with the peelings!

Corers to core apples and pears when preparing those wonderful winter baked fruits.

Olive pitter/cherry stoner – olives are much nicer when you pit them yourself for adding to great summer salads.

A **grater** for grating carrots, beetroot, potatoes, parmesan cheese, nutmeg and many other foods.

A **pastry cutter** for your scones and biscuits and for cutting shapes out of pastry and other foods.

Keeping Knives Sharp

I am much happier in the kitchen when my knives are sharp. When my knives are blunt, I don't cook as fast and I injure myself more.

The most efficient way to keep knives sharp is to sharpen them with a **steel** each time you use them. It takes only about ten seconds once you have mastered the technique.

Hold the clean and dry knife in your better hand and hold the sharpening steel in the other hand. Starting at the base of the blade, stroke the whole length of the blade against the steel at an angle of 15°–20°. You also use most of the length of the steel in the process. Using gentle pressure, repeat the action two or three times on each side of the blade. You can always ask a chef, butcher, parent or friend to show you the technique, which can vary from person to person.

It is also good to sharpen your knives on an **oilstone** two or three times a year. An oilstone is a man-made, hard stone with a very fine finish which gives a smooth, sharp edge to knives.

Using kitchen paper, pat the fine side of the stone with a little vegetable cooking oil or water, then place the stone on a damp tea towel for stability. Angle the blade at 20° against the stone and draw the blade from left to right and back again so as to smooth the rough

19

edge of the blade. Turn the knife over and repeat the process with the other side of the blade. About twenty seconds on each side should do the trick.

Then, about once every 12–18 months, I take my knives to a professional for a serious sharpening and for fixing uneven edges or broken tips. (Look in the Yellow Pages for knife-sharpening professionals.)

Have your scissors and serrated knives sharpened professionally as it is difficult to do a good job on these without being skilled.

Some slotted sharpeners work well, and they are easy to use and come with instructions. They work by drawing the knife through a slot that is lined with hard metal or stone. Light pressure is required. Electric sharpeners based on the same principle can also be helpful.

Storing Knives

Store your good knives in a special wooden knife block with slots for the different knives. Alternatively, store them in slots cut at the rear or side of your work bench, or hold them on metal magnets. Storing sharp knives in a drawer can be dangerous. In general, it is best if sharp blades are not in contact with each other as the friction of metal against metal causes them to become blunt more quickly.

Chopping Boards

Most chopping boards are made of wood or plastic. Wooden boards are the most gentle on your knives but are heavier and a bit more difficult to wash well and remove odours. It is a good idea to have several boards of varying sizes to use for different foods.

Avoid buying boards smaller than 30 cm x 20 cm (12 in x 8 in). Avoid also very thick and very large boards that are heavy and unwieldy to wash well under the tap or in the sink. An ideal wooden board is about 40 cm x 25 cm, (15 in x 9 in) about 2 cm (1 in) thick and made of hard wood.

Wash your boards by brushing with soapy water, then rinse and dry them. Don't soak boards in water.

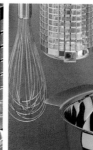

Pots and Pans

Buy pots and pans from large department stores that offer variety, have a large turnover and where the prices are best. Buy sturdy (not necessarily heavy) saucepans with lids that fit well and strong handles.

When deciding what cookware you need, consider what dishes or what kind of food you mostly cook. My recommendation is for a variety of pots and pans – some non-stick, a few stainless-steel and a few cast-iron.

Non-stick cookware is good for low-fat cooking. It's light and the metal under the non-stick coating is usually a good heat conductor. Non-stick saucepans are good for cooking rice dishes, sauces and vegetable casseroles. Non-stick frypans are useful for pan-frying fish fillets, seafood like prawns and scallops, chicken fillets and thighs, and veal slices and cutlets. To keep your non-stick surface longer, use wooden spoons and hard plastic utensils.

Stainless-steel pans are great for cooking pasta or vegetables in a large volume of water and for making soups and stocks. Stainless steel is best used when you are cooking in liquid.

A **stainless-steel steamer** is perfect for cooking vegetables and for keeping them hot, once cooked.

Ovenware and casserole dishes. Most modern metal cookware is both flameproof (okay for cooking on a stove top or element) and ovenproof. Many saucepans, including those with hard plastic handles, are nowadays ovenproof to about 150–200°C (300–400°F) – this is usually indicated on the packaging. Cast-iron pans are heavy and best suited to cooking stews and casseroles on top of the stove or in the oven. Porcelain and glass ovenware are excellent in ovens but can't be used on the top of the stove. If you don't have a flameproof casserole dish, brown food first in a frying pan or wok, then transfer to an ovenproof dish.

A **cast-iron grill** or barbecue plate is excellent for grilling meat, such as chops and steak, for cooking fish such as tuna and salmon, and for vegetables such as eggplant and zucchini. They can be used both on top of the stove or in the oven.

A **wok** is a must in the modern kitchen for stir-fries, quick seafood or chicken curries, noodle dishes, etc. Choose a traditional Chinese iron wok with a close-fitting lid and stir-fry spatula thrown in. If you don't have a wok, a non-stick stir-fry pan (deep frypan) is a good asset and a little easier to use for novice cooks.

I suggest a medium-to-large, deep **baking dish** or **roasting tray**, not too light but not too heavy either. My choice is for a thick, non-stick baking dish that you can use both on top of the stove, under the grill and in the oven. It's useful to have an oven rack that fits in or on your baking dish so the heat can circulate round the roast.

A **flat metal oven tray** is necessary for baking biscuits and pastries, and fish fillets and vegetables.

A **pressure cooker** is a great time saver. I use mine regularly for making soups, stews, bolognese sauce, and, would you believe, risotto! Modern pressure cookers are electric and have a non-stick coating.

Useful Kitchen Utensils

A **salad spinner** to dry washed green leaves, lettuce, rocket and even herbs.

A **mouli** to make vegetable purées and delicious mashed potato.

A **cake rack** to allow family cakes to cool evenly.

A **colander** to drain vegetables and other foods cooked in water.

Glass jars: keep empty jars and their lids for storing nuts, spices, dried fruits, home-made sauces and pastes, such as pesto.

A **rolling pin** for a home-made pizza or a family fruit tart.

A **measuring jug**: with measurements in cups, millilitres and grams, as well as the equivalent in sugar, flour etc.

A few **cake tins** and **lift-out flan tins**: for special treats.

A small **mortar and pestle**: to crush and grind spices.

A set of metric **measuring spoons.**

Scales to measure ingredients for cakes and desserts.

Useful Cooking Terms

Bake: Refers to cooking in the oven.

Baste: To spoon or brush fat or a liquid onto food, such as steak or a roast, during cooking to keep the food moist and to add flavour.

Beat: Mix energetically, using a whisk or electric beater.

Browning: This occurs when foods, such as meat or fish, are placed on medium to high heat in a little oil in a frypan, wok or roasting tray. Done on top of the stove.

Chop: To cut food, like onion or parsley, into very small, regular pieces.

Combine: Two foods or more are combined when they are mixed well together.

Cream: To whisk or beat butter and sugar until soft and smooth.

Dice: To cut vegetables, meat or fruit into small cubes, about 5 mm to 1 cm ($\frac{1}{4}$ to $\frac{1}{2}$ in) square.

Drain: To remove fat or liquid from food.

Drizzle: To pour or spoon a dressing, liquid or fat over food in a fine stream.

Grease: To spread oil, butter or other fat on bakeware to prevent food from sticking.

Grill: To cook under direct heat (electric or gas), or on a barbecue or cast-iron grill.

Heat: To bring food to a temperature that will make it hot.

Julienne: To cut food the size of fine matchsticks.

Knead: To fold and press dough in order to give it elasticity.

Marinade: A seasoning that can be made using spices, herbs, oil or liquid. It helps flavour food and/or tenderise it.

Pan-fry: To cook on medium to high heat in a small amount of fat in a wok or frypan.

Shred: To cut food, such as lettuce or cabbage, into fine strips, using a knife.

Simmer: When food cooks slowly in a liquid or sauce just below or on boiling point.

Stew: To simmer food in a sauce or liquid in a covered pan.

Stir-fry: To cook food in a wok or frypan on medium to high heat in a small or medium quantity of fat while stirring continuously.

Toss: To mix several ingredients with a lifting motion without damaging them.

Whip: To beat food, such as cream, butter or eggs, using a whisk or electric beater, in order to incorporate bubbles of air and increase the volume.

Whisk: To beat food, using a wire whisk, so as to mix or combine.

Zest: To remove in strips the thin, outside layer of lemon or orange rind by using a fine grater or zester.

SOUP

It's easy to learn to make satisfying soups – just be sure to use fresh ingredients, especially for vegetable soups. If you've never made a soup before, start with an easy one, like the Pumpkin Soup or the Simple Leek and Potato Soup. When you feel more confident, try the lovely Minestrone Soup – it's a meal in itself, and a healthy one too!

Pumpkin Soup

An old favourite and simple to make. You can cook it even faster if you use a pressure cooker.

Serves about 4

1 tbsp olive oil
1 brown onion, finely sliced
1 cup diced celery
1 butternut pumpkin, peeled, seeded and diced
about 8 cups chicken stock (see page 40) or water
salt and freshly ground black pepper
1 clove garlic, finely chopped
4 tbsp finely chopped coriander leaves or parsley

Heat the oil in a non-stick saucepan and stir-fry the onion on medium heat for about 5 minutes without browning. Add the celery and stir-fry for 2 minutes. Add the pumpkin, cover with stock or water, and season with salt and pepper. Bring to the boil and simmer for 20 minutes.

Cool slightly and purée in a blender or food processor, adding some boiling water if it is too thick.

Return the soup to the saucepan and reheat.

Stir in the garlic and coriander and serve.

Stocks

See the recipes on pages 40, 41 and 43 for home-made stocks. Most of the soups in this section can be made suitable for vegetarians by using water or vegetable stock instead of meat stock.

If you use commercial stocks, try different varieties to find the one you prefer – finding one you like is a matter of taste. Liquid stocks may not necessarily be better quality – read the labels to see what's in the stock to help you make a decision.

Simple Leek and Potato Soup

This is a good basic soup to learn to make and you can adapt it to your taste or to what you have on hand in the fridge. If possible, use home-made chicken stock instead of water and stock cubes or powder. You may prefer not to blend the soup to a purée and enjoy a coarser-style soup.

Serves about 4

2 medium-sized leeks

1 medium-sized carrot

1 tbsp olive oil or butter

about 8 cups chicken stock (see page 40) or water

2 large potatoes

salt and freshly ground black pepper

1 clove garlic, chopped (optional)

2 tbsp chopped parsley

Trim away the root and the greenest part of the leeks, leaving about 8 cm (3 in) of the green leaves. Cut the leeks into four lengthwise and wash in lukewarm water. Slice the leeks, and peel and slice the carrot.

Heat the oil or butter in a non-stick saucepan. Add the leeks and carrots and stir-fry on a medium heat for 5 minutes without browning. Add the stock or water and stir well.

Peel and dice the potatoes and add to the soup. Cook for a further 20 minutes.

Blend the soup until smooth. If it is too thick, add boiling water.

Just before serving, season to taste with salt and pepper and stir in the garlic and parsley.

Silverbeet Cream Soup

You can replace the silverbeet with spinach, peas or beans, and you can also add a diced potato early in the cooking if you wish to add a little texture to the soup.

Serves 4–6

1 bunch silverbeet

1 tbsp olive oil or butter

1 small brown onion, sliced

1 good tbsp plain flour

2 cups chicken stock (see page 40)

¼ cup milk

salt and freshly ground black pepper

a little grated nutmeg

4 tbsp grated parmesan cheese

Trim off the silverbeet stalks and remove any damaged leaves. Wash the leaves and slice them coarsely. The stalks can be used in a stir-fry dish.

Heat the oil or butter in a large, non-stick saucepan. Add the onion and cook for 2–3 minutes until soft but not coloured. Stir in the flour and cook for 2 minutes more. Whisk in the stock, then add the silverbeet and stir until the soup boils. Cover and simmer for 5 minutes.

Blend to a purée in a blender or processor. Return the soup to the saucepan and add the milk. Reheat without boiling and season to taste with salt and pepper. Add nutmeg, stir in the parmesan and serve.

Corn and Leek Soup

This delicate soup is easily made with the help of canned corn. Leftover roast or boiled chicken can be added to the soup to transform it into a light meal.

Serves 6–8

2 medium-sized leeks

2 medium-sized potatoes

$1/2$ tbsp vegetable oil

6 cups chicken stock (see page 40) or cold water

salt and freshly ground black pepper

400 g (14 oz) can corn kernels

2 pinches of cayenne pepper

1 egg (optional)

3 tbsp snipped chives

Cut the leeks in four lengthwise, leaving the root intact. Wash leeks thoroughly in lukewarm water to flush out dirt. Slice the leeks thinly.

Peel and dice the potatoes.

Heat the oil in a medium, non-stick saucepan on low heat. Add the leeks and stir for about 5 minutes. Add the stock or water and the diced potato. Season with salt and pepper, bring to the boil and cook for about 15 minutes.

Meanwhile, drain the corn.

Blend the leek and potato preparation with a third of the corn to a fine purée. Add the remaining corn and reheat on a low heat. Season with cayenne pepper.

Just before serving, whisk in the egg and sprinkle with chives.

French Provincial Vegetable Soup

This popular thick soup comes from the southern region of France and it is a meal in itself.

Serves 6–8

200 g (7 oz) lean bacon in one piece
  (Ask your butcher or deli to cut it for you.)
4 medium-sized potatoes
1/2 tbsp olive oil
a sprig of fresh thyme, chopped
2 cloves garlic, crushed
8 cups water
400 g (14 oz) can borlotti or other white beans
1/4 cabbage, washed and finely shredded
salt and freshly ground black pepper

Cut the bacon into cubes of approx 1 cm (1/2 in). Peel and dice the potatoes.

Heat the oil in a large non-stick saucepan and stir-fry the bacon for 2 minutes. Stir in the thyme and garlic. Add the potatoes and water and season with salt and pepper. Bring to the boil and cook for 10 minutes.

Add the beans and return to the boil. Add the shredded cabbage, and cook for about 10 minutes or until the cabbage is tender. Serve in bowls over slices of bread.

Rice and Mushroom Soup

This type of soup provides a delicious light meal.

Serves about 4

1 leek

1 carrot

200 g (7 oz) mushrooms

$1/2$ tbsp olive oil

$1/2$ cup brown rice, or white rice if you prefer

5 cups chicken stock (see page 40), vegetable stock (see page 41) or water

a pinch of salt

3 tbsp chopped parsley

freshly ground black pepper

Remove any damaged outer leaves from the leek and cut off most of the tough green part. Chop off the root at the base, then cut the leek in four lengthwise, leaving the base intact. Wash thoroughly in lukewarm water to flush out any dirt. Slice the leek thinly.

Peel the carrot, then cut into small dice. Wash and dice the mushrooms.

Heat the oil in a saucepan and gently fry the leek, carrot and mushroom for a few minutes. Add the rice, stock and salt and cook for 15 minutes or until the rice is done. It takes less time if you use white rice.

Remove half the soup and blend to a purée. Return the soup to the pan and bring to the boil. Before serving, stir in the chopped parsley and season with pepper.

Celery, Sweet Potato and Bean Soup

This easy-to-prepare soup is really nourishing and great for vegetarians provided it's eaten with good bread. The addition of herbs such as coriander, parsley or chives is important for flavour.

Serves 4–6

5 sticks celery

2 medium-sized orange sweet potatoes

1 tbsp olive oil

salt (optional) and freshly ground black pepper

400 g (14 oz) can butter beans or borlotti beans

1 clove garlic, finely chopped

4 tbsp chopped coriander, parsley or chives

Trim off the base of the celery and peel any large stringy sticks. Cut the celery into small pieces. Peel and dice the sweet potatoes.

Heat the oil in a non-stick saucepan. Add the celery and stir on a medium heat for 3 to 4 minutes. Add the sweet potato and cover with water to about 3 cm (1 in) over the vegetables. Season with a little salt and pepper and bring to the boil. Cook for about 20 minutes.

Drain and rinse the beans and then add to the saucepan and simmer for 5 more minutes.

Blend the soup almost to a purée. Add some boiling water if it is too thick. Stir in the garlic and herbs of your choice and serve immediately.

Split Pea and Carrot Soup with Shredded Ham

Plan ahead for this soup and soak the split peas overnight or for about 12 hours. Served with wholesome bread, this soup makes a satisfying meal.

Serves 4–6

1 1/2 cups yellow or green split peas

2 medium-sized carrots

1/2 tbsp olive oil

1/2 brown onion, chopped

12 caraway or cumin seeds

a few sprigs of parsley, a sprig of thyme and 1/2 bay leaf, washed and tied together with kitchen string (bouquet garni)

6 cups chicken stock (see page 40), vegetable stock (see page 41) or cold water

a pinch of salt

4 thin slices ham

freshly ground black pepper

1 clove garlic, finely chopped

3 tbsp chopped parsley

Soak the split peas overnight or for about 12 hours.

Peel and dice the carrots.

Heat the oil in a non-stick saucepan. Fry the onion, carrot and caraway seeds for a few minutes. Add the drained split peas, herbs and stock or water and bring to the boil. Cook for about 30 minutes or until the peas are tender. Halfway through the cooking, season with salt.

Trim the fat from the ham, then cut the ham into small strips.

Remove half the soup and blend to a purée, then return it to the pot. Reheat the soup and season with pepper. Just before serving, add the ham, garlic and parsley.

Minestrone Soup

One of the great soups of the world, minestrone is really a light meal. If the quantities given are too large for you, just halve them. Alternatively, freeze some of the soup once it has cooled.

Serves about 8

2 tbsp olive oil

1 brown onion, diced

2 sticks celery, diced

2 carrots, peeled and diced

1 tsp chopped rosemary

2 rashers bacon, chopped (optional)

2 cloves garlic, crushed

1 tbsp tomato paste

$1/4$ small cabbage, shredded (about 4 cups)

3 medium-sized zucchinis, diced

salt and freshly ground black pepper

1 cup small macaroni or other short pasta, such as vermicelli

2 x 400 g (14 oz) cans cannellini or other white beans, drained

4 tbsp chopped parsley

4 tbsp grated parmesan cheese

Heat the oil in a large saucepan and on a low to medium heat gently fry the onion, celery, carrot, rosemary and bacon for about 5 minutes. Stir in the garlic and tomato paste. Add the cabbage and zucchini, cover with cold water and bring to the boil. Season with salt and pepper and cook for about 20 minutes.

Add the macaroni to the soup, stir well and cook for 5 minutes. Add a little boiling water, if necessary.

Meanwhile, blend half the beans to a purée. Add purée and beans to the soup and boil until the pasta is cooked. Stir in the parsley and serve sprinkled with a little parmesan.

Vegetarian Chickpea Soup

Hearty and satisfying, this soup is a great source of protein. Enjoy it with a good slice of bread.

Serves 4

1 green capsicum
2 tbsp olive oil
1 small brown onion, chopped
$\frac{1}{2}$ tsp mustard seeds
2 cloves garlic, chopped
1 tsp curry powder
400 g (14 oz) can chopped tomatoes
1 tbsp tomato paste
about 4 cups vegetable stock (see page 41) or water
400 g (14 oz) can chickpeas, drained
salt and freshly ground black pepper
2 tbsp finely chopped coriander leaves

Halve, seed, wash and dice the capsicum.

Heat the oil in a large saucepan on a medium heat. Add the onion, mustard seeds, garlic and curry powder and stir for 2 minutes. Add the capsicum and stir for 2 minutes. Add the chopped tomatoes, tomato paste and stock or water, and simmer for 10 minutes.

Blend the drained chickpeas to a purée then stir them into the soup. Season with salt and pepper and simmer until the soup is hot.

Stir in the coriander just before serving.

Cold Summer Vegetable Soup

This makes a refreshing way to eat raw vegetables in summer, and you can adapt the soup by changing the proportions of vegetables.

Serves 4–6

1/2 long continental (telegraph) cucumber

1/2 brown onion, diced

2 cloves garlic, crushed

1/2 green capsicum

4 large, ripe tomatoes

3 tbsp extra virgin olive oil

salt and freshly ground black pepper

a pinch or two of cayenne pepper

6 slices wholemeal bread, crust removed

1 cup vegetable stock (see page 41) or chicken stock (see page 40)

1 tbsp red wine vinegar

4 tbsp finely cut chives

Peel the cucumber and halve it lengthwise. Remove and discard the seeds and dice the cucumber. Place in a large bowl with the onion and garlic.

Halve the capsicum and remove seeds. Wash and dice the capsicum and add to the bowl. Cut the tomatoes into small pieces, removing the core, and add to the bowl.

Add the olive oil, a little salt, pepper and cayenne pepper and toss well. Cover with plastic wrap and refrigerate for 2 hours.

Soak the bread in the stock and vinegar.

Blend the vegetables and bread to a purée in a food processor. Add ice-cold water if the soup is too thick. Serve sprinkled with chives.

Hot Sour Prawn and Flathead Soup with Noodles

Adapt this soup to your taste by using another type of fish and by adding Asian greens, such as Chinese broccoli or cabbage. Tom yum paste and tamarind purée are available from Chinese grocers or in the Asian section of supermarkets.

Serves 4

8 large green prawns

1 tbsp vegetable oil

1 stalk lemongrass, smashed (use the side of a large knife)

1 dried or fresh lime leaf, finely sliced

1 tsp brown sugar

6 cups cold water

$1/2$ cup finely diced celery

2 tsp tom yum paste

20 small mushrooms, halved

$1/2$ tbsp tamarind purée

1 small red chilli, finely sliced

50 g (2 oz) cellophane noodles

200 g (7 oz) flathead fillets, cut into 12 long pieces

1 tbsp fish sauce

juice of $1/2$ lime

$1/2$ cup fresh coriander leaves

4 spring onions, finely sliced

Shell and devein the prawns (see page 186 if you're not sure how to devein prawns), and keep the heads and shells.

Heat the oil in a wok and stir-fry the prawn heads and shells on a high heat for about 4 minutes. Add the lemongrass, lime leaf, sugar and water and bring to a simmer. Cook for 15 minutes.

Strain this liquid into a saucepan, discarding the heads and shells. Bring to the boil, add the celery, tom yum paste and mushrooms and simmer for 5 minutes.

Add the tamarind purée, chilli, noodles, prawn flesh and fish and cook gently for 3 minutes.

Stir in the fish sauce, lime juice, coriander leaves and spring onions and serve.

Winter Fish Soup

Eaten with bread, this makes a nourishing meal. The smoked fish flavour is delicate, and if you make sure there are no bones, some children will love it too. Omit the smoked fish if you prefer.

Serves 4

1 medium-sized leek

2 tbsp olive oil

2 tomatoes, roughly chopped

1 medium-sized zucchini, cut into thin slices

2 medium-sized potatoes, peeled and diced

1 tbsp ground sweet paprika

salt and freshly ground black pepper

6 cups cold water or fish stock (see page 43)

1 smoked rainbow trout (about 400 g or 14 oz), or
    300 g (10 oz) smoked eel

about 300 g (10 oz) firm fish fillets, skinless and boneless

2 cloves garlic, finely chopped

3 tbsp chopped parsley

Remove any damaged leaves from the leek, then trim off the root, keeping about 5 cm (2 in) of the very green part. Cut the leek into quarters lengthwise, leaving the base intact. Wash the leek well in lukewarm water then slice it finely. Discard the base.

Heat the oil in a large, non-stick saucepan or wok. Gently cook the leek for 3 minutes. Stir in the tomatoes, zucchini and potatoes. Add the paprika and season with salt and pepper. Cover with 6 cups of cold water or stock and simmer for 15 minutes.

Meanwhile, skin and bone the trout. Break the flesh up into small pieces. Cut the fresh fish fillets into small cubes.

Stir the fish into the soup and simmer for a further 5 minutes.

Just before serving, stir in the garlic and parsley.

Chicken Stock

You can use the carcass of a cooked chicken but it will give inferior stock. Fresh bones make better, more flavoursome stock than bones from cooked meat.

Chicken stock is the most useful and easy meat stock to prepare. The idea of a stock is to infuse water with strong meat and vegetable flavour. Make a large quantity and freeze it in freezer bags. Chicken stock is used in soups, sauces, casseroles and stews.

Makes about 2 litres (4 pints)

about 2 kg (4 lb) fresh chicken bones (carcass, neck, wings) with as much fat and skin removed as possible, or a whole chicken about 1.8 kg (3½ lb), skin removed

1 large carrot, cut into 1 cm (½ in) slices

1 large onion, quartered

2 sticks celery, cut into 3 cm (1 in) pieces

1 clove

6 sprigs of parsley, 1 sprig of thyme and a small bayleaf, washed and tied together with kitchen string

1 tsp sea salt

6 black peppercorns, crushed

Place the chicken bones or the whole, skinned chicken in a large saucepan or stock pot. Add the carrot, onion, celery, clove and herbs and season with salt and pepper. Cover with cold water and bring to the boil. Reduce the heat and simmer for 45 minutes, skimming off the surface foam two or three times during the cooking.

Strain the stock and discard the bones and vegetables, although you can eat the vegetables if you wish. If you have used a whole chicken, you could use the meat in a salad (see page 118), a risotto (see page 100) or a curry (see page 205).

When the stock is cold, remove any fat from the surface. You can store the stock for 3–4 days in the refrigerator or in the freezer for up to 6 months.

Vegetable Stock

This stock is perfect to use in a vegetarian risotto (see page 98).

Makes about 2 litres (4 pints)

1 brown onion

2 carrots

2 sticks celery

1 small leek, washed

1 tbsp olive oil

about 2$\frac{1}{2}$ litres (5 pints) cold water

2 sprigs of thyme

4 sprigs of parsley

1 clove

salt and freshly ground black pepper

Peel the onion and carrots and slice them finely. Slice the celery and leek.

Heat the oil in a non-stick saucepan and stir-fry the onion until lightly browned. Add the carrot, celery and leek and stir-fry for about 3 minutes. Add the water, thyme, parsley and clove and season with salt and pepper. Simmer uncovered for about 20 minutes.

Strain the broth and allow it to cool before storing.

The stock can be stored in the refrigerator for 2–3 days or in the freezer for up to 2 months.

Fat Content of
Some Common Foods

All oils (olive, safflower, peanut, etc.)	100%
Butter	about 85%
Lard, dripping, suet	about 100%
Margarine	about 85%
Most nuts (macadamias, hazelnuts, almonds)	35–60%
Puff pastry, shortcrust and sweet pastry, strudel	about 40%
Rich cream	48% maximum
Pure cream	35% minimum
Thickened cream	35%
Reduced cream	25% minimum
Light cream and sour cream	18% minimum
Extra light cream	12% minimum
Milk	about 4%
Low-fat milk	about 2%
Skim milk	less than 1%
Powdered milk (not reconstituted)	about 28%
Plain yoghurt	about 4%
Greek-style yoghurt	about 10%
Goat's milk	about 5%
Cheeses – most	25–35%
Cheddar	about 35%
Fetta	about 15%
Swiss-style	about 25%
Mascarpone	about 50%
Mozzarella, bocconcini	about 25%
Parmesan	about 30%
Neufchâtel	about 25%
Cream cheese	about 30%
Ricotta	about 10%
Cottage cheese (low-fat cream cheese, quark)	about 2–10%
Brie, camembert	about 25–30%
Blue vein	about 30%

Fish Stock

Once you have become a confident cook, a recipe like this one is precious, because it has so many uses. It can be the basis for a soup, risotto or seafood sauce or you can poach a fish in it. Ask your fishmonger for very clean bones and heads (no gills, scales or guts) of saltwater fish. River fish do not make good fish stock.

Makes 2 litres (4 pints) of strong fish stock

5 sprigs of parsley

2 sprigs of thyme

$1/2$ bay leaf

1 large carrot

1 large stick celery

1 medium-sized brown onion

20 g ($2/3$ oz) butter or 1 tbsp vegetable oil

about 1 kg (2 lb) cleaned saltwater fish bones, e.g. snapper, John Dory, flathead, cut into about 10 cm (4 in) pieces

$1/2$ cup dry white wine

salt

Tie the parsley, thyme and bay leaf together with string to form a bouquet garni, or you can leave them loose.

Wash the carrot and celery and slice them into small pieces. Chop the onion into small pieces.

Heat the butter in a large saucepan on a medium heat and gently stir-fry the vegetables for about 5 minutes. Add the herbs, fish bones and the wine. Cover with at least 8 cups of cold water and season with a little salt. Bring to the boil and simmer for 20 minutes.

Strain the stock through a fine strainer and discard the bones.

If you are not going to use the stock soon, you can reduce it further by boiling it down which will make it easier to store. Allow it to cool and, when it is cold, remove any fat from the surface. Store in the refrigerator for 2 or 3 days or in the freezer for up to 2 months.

SNACKS

People in our modern world are becoming more and more overweight because there is an imbalance between what we eat and the energy we burn. Of course, rich snacks and lack of exercise are often responsible for our being overweight. It's best to have a good breakfast, and a nourishing lunch and dinner, and to avoid snacks in between (unless recommended by a health professional). When you do snack, choose carefully, and try to make the snack an opportunity to eat what you have missed in your regular meals during the day, for example, fruit, carbohydrate or vegetables, so that you achieve a balanced diet as far as possible. And whatever you do, choose snacks that are low in fat and sugar. Personally, for a snack, I love to have a soft-boiled egg, or a pan-fried egg done in a minimum of fat, and eaten with a piece of wholemeal toast.

Guacamole

Serve this dip with sticks of carrot, capsicum, celery, fennel, cucumber or cauliflower, or with nachos or a bread of your choice.

Serves 2–4

1 medium-sized ripe avocado
juice of $\frac{1}{4}$ lemon
3 drops of tabasco
salt and freshly ground black pepper
1 tomato
about 1 tbsp finely chopped onion
2 tbsp coriander leaves, finely sliced
1 tbsp sour cream

Halve the avocado, remove the stone and scoop out the flesh. Place the avocado flesh in a bowl and mash with a fork. Season with the lemon juice, tabasco and a little salt and pepper.

Core and halve the tomato and squeeze out the seeds. Dice the tomato and add to the bowl with the onion, coriander and sour cream. Combine gently and either serve immediately or refrigerate until 10 minutes before serving.

Hummus

This classic Middle Eastern vegetarian dip is delicious with raw vegetables and bread. It makes a great sandwich spread and is perfect for an antipasto platter.

Serves 6–10

200 g (7 oz) dried chickpeas or 2 x 400 g (14 oz) cans cooked
   chickpeas, drained

1 tsp ground cumin

3 tbsp tahini (sesame seed paste)

juice of 1 lemon

3 tbsp water

1/2 tsp salt

freshly ground black pepper

1 clove garlic, very finely chopped (optional)

If using dried chickpeas, soak the chickpeas for 24 hours in about four times their volume of water. Drain and rinse. Place the chickpeas in a large pot of cold, unsalted water. Bring them to the boil, then simmer for about 2 hours or until they are tender. Allow to cool.

Drain the cooked or tinned chickpeas and blend to a fine purée. Add the cumin, tahini, lemon juice, water, salt and pepper, then blend again. Refrigerate the hummus. Just before serving, add the chopped garlic.

Tuna and Olive Spread

This is a version of the French olive paste called 'tapenade'. It goes well with good breads, for example, wholemeal, wholegrain, olive or walnut bread, and also with raw vegetable sticks – try it with carrots, cucumber, celery and cauliflower.

Serves 2–4

200 g (7 oz) can tuna in oil, drained
2 anchovy fillets
20 black olives, pitted
1 clove garlic, crushed
2 tsp lemon juice
1 tsp Dijon mustard (optional)
2 tbsp olive oil
freshly ground black pepper

Place the tuna, anchovy fillets, olives, garlic, lemon juice and mustard in a food processor and blend until the mixture is spreadable. Add the oil and a little pepper and blend briefly, just to combine.

Transfer to a bowl and refrigerate. Take out 10 minutes before you are ready to serve.

Yoghurt, Tahini and Mint Dip

Smooth and easy to prepare, this dip is lovely with spicy meatballs such as koftas, or with grilled fish or raw vegetables.

Serves about 4

4 tbsp Greek-style yoghurt
1 tbsp tahini (sesame seed paste)
5 mint leaves, finely chopped
salt and freshly ground black pepper
a few drops of lemon juice (optional)

In a bowl whisk together the yoghurt, tahini and mint. Season with salt and pepper and lemon juice. Refrigerate if not using immediately.

Beans and Parsley on Toast

Great as a snack or lunch, especially for vegetarians. Use your favourite cooked beans, e.g. cannellini, butter beans, kidney beans.

Serves 4

2 cups cooked beans, home-cooked or canned

1 tbsp olive oil

2 tbsp chopped parsley

1 small clove garlic, finely chopped

salt and freshly ground black pepper

4 large slices of wholemeal or wholegrain bread

Drain the cooked beans and rinse them under cold water for a few seconds.

Heat the oil in a non-stick pan and heat the beans on a medium heat. Stir in the parsley and garlic and season with a little salt and pepper. Serve on toast.

Hints for People with Diabetes

Have regular meals and don't miss any meals.

Cook using a minimum of fat, trim meat of fat before cooking and enjoy low-fat dairy products, e.g. yoghurt, milk, cheese.

Eat plenty of vegetables.

Learn to manage your weight and exercise regularly.

Eat wholegrain bread, rice and other foods.

Enjoy oats or bran for breakfast.

Eat foods that are low in added sugar, and minimise the consumption of biscuits and cakes.

Drink alcohol in moderation, drink only when you eat and avoid fortified liqueurs.

Avoid sweetened or fizzy drinks.

Artichoke and Prosciutto Sandwich on Olive Bread

Olive bread, which is now one of the most popular gourmet breads, is delicious with all kinds of Mediterranean fillings, such as grilled vegetables, canned fish (sardines, tuna, mackerel) or cold meats such as lamb or prosciutto.

Makes 1 sandwich

1 or 2 artichoke hearts in oil
4 or 5 rocket leaves or other greens
2 thin slices prosciutto
2 thick slices olive bread

Drain the artichoke hearts and cut them into 5 mm ($^1/4$ in) slices.

Place the artichoke slices on one piece of bread and top with half the washed and drained rocket. Top with the prosciutto and the remaining rocket and artichoke hearts. Close the sandwich, cut it in half and have a feast!

Alternatively, wrap the sandwich in plastic wrap and refrigerate until required.

Grilled Vegetable
and Ricotta Sandwich

Many delis now sell grilled vegetables, such as eggplant, zucchini, artichoke hearts and capsicum, preserved in oil. Alternatively, grill your own selection (see page 144).

Makes 2 sandwiches

4 large slices wholemeal, olive or herb bread

a selection of grilled vegetables,
   e.g. 2 slices eggplant, 4 slices zucchini, 2 slices capsicum

80 g (3 oz) fresh ricotta

Toast the four slices of bread.

Spread a little ricotta on each slice of warm toast, then top two of the slices with the grilled vegetables. Season with salt and pepper and close the sandwiches. Cut each sandwich in half and consume immediately.

Spicy Sardine, Rocket and Carrot Sandwich

Replace the sardines with mackerel or salmon, if you wish, and vary the vegetables by using sliced tomatoes, lettuce or avocado.

Makes 2 sandwiches

120 g (4 oz) can sardines in oil

salt and freshly ground black pepper

a pinch of cayenne pepper or $1/2$ green chilli, finely sliced (optional)

2 tbsp finely chopped coriander or parsley

4 slices of rye bread, or bread of your choice

$1/2$ cup grated carrot

a handful of rocket leaves, washed

Using a fork, mash the sardines in half their oil on a plate. Throw away the remaining oil. Season with salt, pepper, cayenne and the chopped coriander.

Spread the mashed sardines on the four slices of bread. Top two of the slices with grated carrot and rocket. Place the other slices of bread on top, cut each sandwich in half and serve.

Pita Pocket with Vegetables and Cheese

Select a wholemeal pita pocket if you need more fibre in your diet. You can be creative with your fillings but avoid using ingredients that are too moist, such as a runny dressing, or tomatoes with their seeds. Pita pockets make a good lunch box option.

Serves 1

2 tsp mayonnaise or Greek-style plain yoghurt

3 tbsp grated carrot

$1/4$ avocado, diced

1 slice cooked beetroot, diced

2 tbsp grated cheese of your choice

salt and freshly ground black pepper

1 pita pocket bread

Place the mayonnaise in a bowl. Stir in the carrot, avocado, beetroot and cheese and season to taste with salt and pepper.

Spoon this filling into the pocket bread and eat straight away or wrap in greaseproof paper, foil or plastic film and store in the refrigerator.

Ham and Sun-dried Tomato Muffins

Fun to make, these muffins are really tasty and a great place to start teaching kids to cook.

Makes 12 muffins

3 cups self-raising flour
$\frac{1}{2}$ tsp salt
$\frac{1}{2}$ tsp freshly ground black pepper
$\frac{1}{2}$ tsp mustard powder
2 small eggs
80 g ($2\frac{1}{2}$ oz) butter, melted
2 cups buttermilk
$1\frac{1}{2}$ cups tasty cheese, grated
200 g (7 oz) ham, finely diced
$\frac{1}{3}$ bunch fresh chives, finely cut (about $\frac{1}{2}$ cup)
8 sun-dried tomatoes, diced

Preheat the oven to 200°C (400°F).

Grease a 12-muffin tray or 12 muffin cups with butter.

Sift the flour into a large mixing bowl. Add the salt, pepper and mustard powder and stir using a wooden spoon.

Crack the eggs into a small bowl, stir with a fork to break the yolks and mix lightly.

Melt the butter in a small pan on a low heat or in the microwave.

Add the eggs, melted butter and buttermilk to the flour and stir until the mixture is combined, but don't overmix. Gently stir in the cheese, ham, chives and sun-dried tomatoes.

Spoon the mixture into the muffin tray and bake in the preheated oven for 20–25 minutes.

Cool the muffins on a rack for 5–10 minutes before serving.

Pan-fried Eggs
with Peperonata

This popular dish made up of eggs served with a Mediterranean vegetable dish called peperonata, is really satisfying and easy to prepare. It can be made for one person with two eggs, or for two people with four eggs.

Serves 2

$\frac{1}{2}$ tbsp olive oil

$\frac{1}{2}$ red capsicum, sliced

$\frac{1}{4}$ brown onion, sliced

$\frac{1}{2}$ clove garlic, chopped

a pinch of dried oregano

1 small zucchini, sliced

1 small, long eggplant or $\frac{1}{4}$ large eggplant, sliced

1 tomato, quartered

salt and freshly ground black pepper

4 eggs

Heat the oil in a medium-sized, non-stick frypan. Add the capsicum and onion and fry gently for about 5 minutes. Add the garlic, oregano, zucchini, eggplant and tomato. Increase the heat and cook for about 10 minutes, covered with foil. When cooked, season with salt and pepper.

Make four hollows in the vegetables and break the eggs into them. Cook until the eggs are ready. Serve with some good, tasty bread.

Potato and Ham Omelette

This is an omelette in the Spanish style. It's *much* easier to prepare if you use a non-stick frypan.

Serves 2

1 medium-sized potato
1 tbsp olive oil
¼ brown onion, finely sliced
2 tbsp chopped parsley
1 or 2 slices ham, finely shredded
4 eggs
salt and freshly ground black pepper

Peel the potato, quarter it lengthwise, then cut it into thin slices, about 2 mm (⅛ in) thick.

Heat half the oil in a small or medium-sized non-stick frypan and cook the onion and potato on a medium heat until the potato is cooked through. Add the remaining oil and stir well. Add the parsley and ham.

Beat the eggs in a bowl and season with salt and pepper. Add the beaten eggs to the pan and shake it gently to allow the egg to run under the potato. Lower the heat and cook until the egg is almost set.

Carefully turn the omelette over and briefly cook the second side (this step may not be necessary if you are using a wide pan).

Carefully cut the omelette in half using a wooden or plastic spoon and serve. It is delicious served with a green salad.

If you find turning the omelette difficult, put a dinner plate over the frypan and, holding onto the plate, invert the pan and then slide the omelette back into the pan cooked side up.

Asian-style Omelette

This style of tasty omelette is often served for breakfast in Asian hotels.

Serves 3

6 free-range eggs

salt and freshly ground black pepper

2 spring (green) onions, finely sliced

3 tbsp coriander leaves, finely sliced

1 tbsp vegetable oil

$\frac{1}{2}$ brown onion, diced

$\frac{1}{2}$ medium green or red chilli, finely sliced

1 cup bean sprouts, roots removed

Break the eggs into a bowl. Season with salt and pepper and stir in the spring onion and coriander.

Heat the oil in a large non-stick frypan. Add the onion and chilli and stir-fry for 2 minutes. Add the bean sprouts and stir-fry for almost a minute before adding the seasoned eggs. Cook on a high heat, stirring to ensure the mixture cooks evenly. Serve immediately.

To prepare spring onions, first trim off the root, then cut off about 2 cm (1 in) of the green leaves. Remove or trim any damaged parts, then rinse the onion.

Mixed Vegetable Pancakes

Vegetarians will love these pancakes served with a tangy salad. You can use all kinds of vegetables as long as they are cut into small pieces, the size of a corn kernel, and pre-cooked.

Makes about 8 small pancakes

$1/2$ cup self-raising flour

1 small egg

salt and freshly ground black pepper

$1/2$ cup milk or soy milk

a pinch of cayenne pepper

$1/2$ cup cooked peas

$1/2$ cup cooked corn kernels

2 tbsp chopped parsley, coriander leaves or tarragon

1 tsp olive oil

Place the flour in a bowl and make a hollow in the centre. Break the egg into the hollow and season the egg with a little salt and pepper. Add half the milk and mix it well with the egg, before slowly incorporating the flour. Add the remaining milk and stir until smooth.

Leave the batter to rest in the refrigerator for about 20 minutes, then strain it into another bowl. Add the cayenne pepper, peas, corn kernels and herbs and mix well.

Heat the oil in a large, non-stick frying pan. Spoon in the equivalent of about 2 tablespoons of batter per pancake, making four pancakes to start with. Cook the first side on a medium heat for about 1 minute, then carefully turn the pancakes and cook the second side. Remove from the pan and cook the remaining pancakes. Serve nice and hot.

Ham and Onion Pancakes

Makes 12–16 pancakes

150 g (5 oz) plain flour
100 g (3$\frac{1}{2}$ oz) self-raising flour
$\frac{1}{2}$ tsp salt
$\frac{1}{4}$ tsp ground sweet (mild) paprika
pinch of chilli powder
freshly ground black pepper
2 eggs
about 3 cups milk
10 spring (green) onions, finely cut
200 g (7 oz) ham, finely shredded
$\frac{1}{2}$ tbsp vegetable oil
1 tbsp butter

Place both types of flour, salt, paprika, chilli and pepper in a bowl. Make a well in the centre, then pour in the eggs and a third of the milk. Whisk the egg and milk together, then gradually incorporate the flour, slowly whisking in the remaining milk to form a smooth batter. There may be some milk left over. Refrigerate for 20 minutes, then strain.

Add the spring onion and ham to the pancake batter.

Heat the oil and butter on a medium heat in a medium-sized non-stick frypan. When the butter turns golden, whisk it into the batter.

Return the pan to a medium heat and pour in enough batter to thinly cover the base of the pan. When the top half of the pancake starts to dry, turn it over and cook the second side. When cooked, transfer to a plate and repeat until all the batter is used up. If the pancakes start to stick, add a little butter to the pan.

Mexican Corn with Bacon

Mexican food is spicy but doesn't need to be very hot to be enjoyable.

Serves 2

2 whole corn cobs

½ tbsp olive oil

2 rashers bacon, trimmed of fat and cut into long strips

a pinch of cumin seeds

3 tbsp Italian-style tomato sauce, bottled or home-made
  (see page 84)

a pinch of chilli powder or cayenne pepper

1 tsp butter

freshly ground black pepper

2 tbsp finely sliced coriander or parsley leaves

Strip the corn cobs of their leaves and silk and wash the corn. Cook the cobs for about 5 minutes in a large amount of salted boiling water until tender, then drain.

Meanwhile, heat the oil in a non-stick pan and cook the bacon and cumin seeds for 1 minute. Add the tomato sauce and chilli powder and season with butter, salt and pepper. Reheat.

Add the drained whole cobs to the pan and coat with the sauce. Sprinkle the coriander leaves on top and serve.

How to Keep Your Weight Down

To lose weight, most people should eat *better* rather than eat *less*.

Eat high-fibre foods, such as bread, cereal, vegetables.

Eat more vegetables.

Trim meat of fat before cooking.

Cook using a minimum of fat – non-stick cookware helps with this.

Avoid deep-fried foods, such as chips, fish in batter, etc.

Eat at regular times and don't miss any meals.

Stop eating as soon as you feel full and eat slowly – when you eat quickly, it is easy to feel full when it is too late.

Share meals with others, rather than eating alone.

Recognise your bad eating habits.

Exercise regularly to stay fit.

Save rich desserts, like cakes, ice-cream and pastries, for special occasions.

Quick Pizza Dough

This simple recipe is ideal for a quick family pizza or as a snack. It is not as crisp as a traditional pizza dough. I usually prefer Greek-style yoghurts which have a smoother, richer texture than plain natural yoghurts.

Makes 1 small pizza or 6 wedges

1 cup self-raising flour
$^1/_4$ tsp salt
about 4 tbsp natural yoghurt

Combine the flour, salt and yoghurt in a bowl until a soft dough forms. You may need to add a bit more yoghurt if it is too dry to form a ball, or some extra flour if it is too soft. Don't knead the dough – just let it rest for a few minutes while you prepare the topping.

Roll out the dough very thinly and place on a greased pizza tray.

Vegetarian Pizza (without Cheese)

For those allergic to dairy foods, for those keeping an eye on their cholesterol level, or for those simply wanting a delicious vegetarian pizza.

Makes 1 medium-sized pizza

2 tbsp olive oil

1/2 capsicum, very finely sliced

4 mushrooms, finely sliced

1 small zucchini, finely sliced

salt and freshly ground black pepper

10 basil leaves, chopped

1/2 clove garlic, finely chopped

1 tsp dried oregano

a pinch of cayenne pepper

1 medium-sized pizza base, home-made (see page 65) or from the supermarket

4 tbsp Italian-style tomato sauce, bottled or home-made (see page 84)

1 tbsp pepitas (pumpkin seeds)

Preheat the oven to 220°C (425°F).

Heat half the oil in a non-stick frypan or wok and stir-fry the capsicum for 3 minutes. Add the mushroom and zucchini and cook for a few minutes until softened. Drain off any excess moisture and season the vegetables with salt and pepper.

In a small bowl, combine the remaining oil with the basil, garlic, oregano and cayenne pepper. Spread this over the pizza base, then top with the vegetables. Spoon the tomato sauce over and scatter the pepitas on top. Bake in the preheated oven for about 10 minutes or until the base is cooked.

Cut the pizza into wedges and serve.

Quick Pizza with Capsicum, Olives and Fetta

Makes a satisfying light meal or snack. Make sure you cook the pizza in a very hot oven. You need a small pizza tray or flat oven tray.

Serves 1 or 2 (6 wedges)

1 tbsp olive oil
1 clove garlic, finely chopped
1 quantity quick pizza dough (see page 65)
about ¾ capsicum, finely sliced
about 12 black olives, pitted and halved
about 80 g (2½ oz) cubed fetta cheese

Preheat the oven to 250°C (475°F).

Mix the olive oil with the garlic.

Roll out the pizza dough very thinly and lay on an oiled pizza tray. Brush the dough with the mixture of oil and garlic. Scatter the capsicum on top and dot with the olives and fetta.

Cook in the preheated oven for 10–15 minutes or until the dough has browned underneath.

PASTA & RICE

Pasta and rice dishes are filling, popular with young people and mostly easy to prepare. Timing the cooking of pasta and rice is important and the recipe is only a guide. But avoid overcooking, as pasta and rice can become mushy. Use a timer to remind you when to test the food by tasting to see if it's cooked. It's a very good habit for a cook to test food before stopping the cooking or serving the food.

Farfalle (Butterfly Pasta) Carbonara

Carbonara is one of the richest pasta sauces, so a light coating is enough to season the pasta.

Serves 2

150 g (5 oz) dry farfalle
2 lean slices bacon
1 tsp red wine vinegar
2 tbsp cream
2 tbsp grated parmesan cheese
1 egg yolk
freshly ground black pepper
2 tbsp chopped parsley

Bring a large pot of lightly salted water to the boil, then cook the pasta in the boiling water until al dente. Drain the pasta in a colander in the sink.

While the pasta is cooking, chop the bacon into very small pieces.

Heat a non-stick frypan and on a medium heat fry the bacon for 2 minutes. Transfer the bacon to a small bowl. Add the vinegar to the frypan, then add the cream and parmesan and reheat.

Add the hot, drained pasta and the egg yolk to the pan and toss well so that the sauce coats the pasta. Season with pepper, add the bacon and parsley, and serve immediately.

Pasta with Mixed Vegetables

Try to include at least three different vegetables in this dish as well as a herb such as parsley, basil or coriander. Choose your favourite pasta, for example, spaghetti, penne or fettuccine.

Serves 2

1 tbsp olive oil

½ capsicum, finely sliced

6 mushrooms, sliced

½ cup Italian-style tomato sauce, bottled or home-made
   (see page 84)

1 cup cooked peas or other green vegetable

salt and freshly ground black pepper

200 g (7 oz) pasta of your choice

1 tbsp pine nuts

1 tbsp chopped parsley

½ small clove garlic, chopped

2 tbsp grated parmesan cheese (optional)

Heat half the oil in a non-stick frypan or wok, then stir-fry the capsicum for 2 minutes. Add the mushrooms and stir-fry for 3 minutes. Add the tomato sauce and peas and reheat for 2 minutes. Season with salt and pepper.

Cook the pasta according to the packet instructions.

Drain the pasta and add it to the vegetables. Add the pine nuts, parsley, garlic and remaining oil and toss very gently to coat the pasta. Reheat and serve, sprinkled with parmesan.

How to Cook Pasta

Bring a large amount of lightly salted water to the boil. As a guide, you need about 2 litres (4 pints) of water to cook spaghetti for two people, about 3 litres (6½ pints) of water for four people, 4 litres (8½ pints) for six people. You need less water when you cook short pasta.

Once the pasta has been placed in boiling water, stir it briefly to prevent sticking. Bring the water back to a gentle boil.

Fresh pasta takes less time to cook than dried pasta. Ask for an idea of the cooking time when you buy fresh pasta – some types take only 2–3 minutes. An estimated cooking time is usually printed on the packet of dried pasta.

When pasta is just cooked, it is still a little firm and is just moist in the centre (al dente). To do a taste test, take a piece of pasta from the water using tongs. Cool it under cold water then bite into it to gauge how cooked it is.

When the pasta is cooked, place a colander in the sink. Add about half a cup of cold water to the pasta pot to stop further cooking, then drain the pasta into the colander and shake it gently to get rid of any water.

Toss the pasta with seasoning or sauce in a saucepan or bowl.

Popular Pasta Shapes and Varieties

Angel's Hair (capelli d'angelo) is a long, thin pasta used in European and Asian-style soups. It's also nice in a salad with a soy sauce dressing (see page 131).

Bucatini is hollow spaghetti, delicious with meaty sauces and plenty of chopped parsley.

Conchiglie are shaped like shells. The tiny ones are great in soups, while the large ones go well with a meaty or seafood sauce.

Couscous – yes, it is a pasta. Like the others it's made with flour and water; it's just a different shape.

Farfalle, shaped like bowties or butterflies, are popular with children and nice added to a saucy casserole or stew, or in a minestrone.

Fettuccine is long and flat like a ribbon. This is fantastic as a pasta for special occasions, especially when fresh. Great with prawns and other seafood.

Gnocchi look like dumplings and come in several varieties, the most popular being made with mashed potato and flour. Some are made with semolina. Delicious with Italian tomato sauce and grated parmesan.

Lasagna is very thin rectangles or squares of pasta. Lasagna sheets come either dry, fresh or instant (pre-cooked). Look for instructions on the packaging. Fresh lasagna sheets give the most delicious result.

Linguine is flat, narrow and long, used like spaghetti and is better with delicate rather than with chunky sauces.

Long fusilli look like long corkscrews and provide a robust texture. Great with chunky sauces.

Macaroni is a family favourite. These small hollow tubes come in different lengths. Delicious served au gratin or in stews, soups and chunky sauces.

Penne is another superb family tubular pasta. I like to serve penne as a garnish with saucy chicken or rabbit dishes. The kids love them with a little olive oil and grated parmesan.

Ravioli – these filled squares make an easy, delicious meal when bought fresh from the pasta shop. Season them simply with a little Italian tomato sauce, olive oil, chopped parsley, garlic and grated parmesan.

Ruote de carro or 'cartwheel' pasta is lovely with a sauce and with small ingredients that become trapped in the pasta. Popular with children.

Spaghetti, with its long, thin, round shape, is fun to eat. Great with pesto, bolognese and carbonara sauce. Another favourite with kids.

Tagliatelle are long, flat ribbons about 1 cm ($^1/_2$ in) wide. Very satisfying as a main course and great with bolognaise sauce.

Tortellini are a small, folded pasta, shaped like a navel, stuffed with seasoned minced meat. Often cooked and served in a broth or soup, or with a sauce.

Penne with Olives, Anchovies, Tomato and Parsley

This is a version of the sauce Italians call puttanesca – a 'quickie' sauce! Penne are the short tubular pasta that everyone likes.

Serves 4

400 g (14 oz) penne
salt
2 cloves garlic
4 anchovy fillets
400 g (14 oz) can diced or crushed tomatoes
about 200 g (7 oz) pitted black olives
2 tbsp olive oil
4 tbsp chopped parsley
freshly ground black pepper
freshly grated parmesan cheese

Cook the penne in a large pot of salted, boiling water. When the pasta is just cooked, add half a cup of cold water to the pot, then drain the pasta in a colander standing in the sink.

While the pasta is cooking, finely chop the garlic and the anchovy fillets, and cut the olives into small pieces.

Heat the oil in a non-stick pan and stir-fry the garlic and anchovies on a medium heat for 10 seconds. Add the tomato and olives and bring the sauce quickly to the boil on a high heat. Stir in the parsley and season with pepper. Mix the sauce with the cooked pasta before serving with grated parmesan.

Tagliatelle with Amatriciana Sauce

Depending on whom you're cooking for, choose a hot or mild salami. The sauce can be prepared in advance, even the day before.

Serves 2 for a main course

1 clove garlic
about ¼ brown onion
½ small red chilli (or less)
10 thin slices hot or mild salami
1 tbsp olive oil
1 cup diced, canned tomatoes (or fresh ones)
200 g (7 oz) tagliatelle or 150 g (5 oz) fresh tagliatelle
salt
3 tbsp chopped parsley
grated parmesan cheese (optional)

Chop the garlic and onion and finely slice the chilli. Cut each salami slice into four pieces.

Heat the oil in a non-stick pan and stir-fry the onion, garlic and chilli on a medium heat for 2 minutes. Add the salami and stir-fry for 1 minute. Add the tomato and simmer for about 5 minutes.

Cook the pasta until al dente in plenty of boiling salted water. Drain the pasta well, then toss it with the hot sauce. Stir in the chopped parsley and serve with a little grated parmesan.

Fettuccine with Tuna and Olives

This quick pasta dish makes a meal when served with a green or mixed salad.

Serves 2

salt

200 g (7 oz) fresh or dried fettuccine

200 g (7 oz) can tuna in oil

1 clove garlic, chopped

2–3 tbsp finely sliced parsley or basil

freshly ground black pepper

12 black or green olives

a few shavings of parmesan cheese

Bring a large pot of salted water to the boil and cook the pasta until just done. Drain the pasta and place in a saucepan. Gently toss the pasta with the tuna, garlic and basil or parsley. Season with pepper and top with olives and parmesan cheese shavings.

Macaroni au Gratin

This family classic is rich but delicious, and a great way to use up leftover pasta. I enjoy it with sautéed spinach with a touch of garlic.

Food that is cooked 'au gratin' is topped with breadcrumbs or a sauce then placed under the grill to brown lightly on top.

Serves 2

about 150 g (5 oz) macaroni or about 3 cups cooked macaroni

oil to grease the gratin dish

3 tbsp cream

1 egg yolk

$1/2$ tsp ground sweet paprika

a large pinch of curry powder

freshly ground black pepper

3 tbsp grated Swiss-style cheese

2 tbsp dried breadcrumbs

Cook the pasta in a large quantity of salted boiling water. Drain the pasta well and place in a greased gratin dish.

Preheat the grill.

In a small bowl, mix the cream, egg yolk, paprika, curry powder and a little pepper. Spoon this evenly over the hot pasta and sprinkle the top with grated cheese and breadcrumbs. Place under the hot grill long enough to melt and lightly brown the cheese and breadcrumbs. Serve immediately.

Roast Pumpkin
and Ricotta Pasta

Sweet and soft and a perfect match for pasta, this recipe allows
the pumpkin to keep its concentrated flavour.

Serves 2

2 cups butternut pumpkin cut into 2 cm (1 in) cubes

2 tbsp olive oil

salt and freshly ground black pepper

$1/2$ tsp ground sweet paprika

200 g (7 oz) short pasta, e.g. penne, farfalle

1 small clove garlic, finely chopped

10 basil leaves, finely sliced

$1/2$ cup crumbled ricotta

1 tbsp roasted pine nuts (or walnuts)

Preheat the oven to 220°C (425°F).

In a bowl, toss the pumpkin with half the oil and season with
salt, pepper and paprika. Place the seasoned pumpkin in a
non-stick roasting tray and roast in the preheated oven until
soft (about 15–20 minutes).

Meanwhile, cook the pasta in a large amount of salted boiling
water until al dente.

Drain the pasta and transfer to a bowl. Add the garlic, basil,
pumpkin and the remaining oil and toss very gently. Serve on
plates, top with the crumbled ricotta and sprinkle with pine nuts.

Vegetable Lasagna

Lasagna is great
served the next
day. Before
storing leftovers
in the fridge,
cover the dish
with plastic film
to avoid the food
drying out.

This beautiful lasagna takes about 2 hours to prepare, including cooking time. Make the white sauce first.

Serves 6

1 quantity of white sauce (see page 170)

3 tbsp olive oil

1 small brown onion, diced

1 tbsp finely chopped thyme

1 red capsicum, halved, seeded and diced

1 medium-sized eggplant, diced

2 medium-sized zucchinis, diced

2½ cups Italian-style tomato sauce, bottled or home-made (see page 84)

salt and freshly ground black pepper

1 clove garlic, chopped

300 g (10 oz) fresh baby spinach, well washed and drained

a pinch of ground nutmeg

a little extra olive oil

about 500 g (1 lb) instant lasagna sheets (or enough for 4 layers)

3 tbsp grated parmesan cheese

Heat two-thirds of the olive oil in a medium-sized saucepan and stir-fry the onion, thyme and capsicum for about 4 minutes. Add the eggplant and zucchini and stir-fry for 5 minutes. Add the tomato sauce and simmer for 15 minutes.

Heat the remaining olive oil in a large pan or wok. Stir in the garlic and spinach and cook until the spinach is soft. Season with salt, pepper and nutmeg. Drain in a colander.

Brush a lasagna dish, large enough for 6 people (e.g. 20 cm x 30 cm, 8 x 12 in), with olive oil. Preheat the oven to 150°C (300°F).

Line the base of the dish with sheets of instant lasagna.
On top, spread a thin layer of white sauce and half the spinach.
Add another layer of sheets of instant lasagna and a thin layer of white sauce. Top with a 2 cm (1 in) layer of mixed vegetables,

another layer of lasagna sheets, then more white sauce, spinach, another layer of lasagna sheets and the remaining white sauce.

Sprinkle with grated parmesan and bake in the preheated oven for about 40 minutes. Remove from the oven and rest for 5 minutes before serving.

Pantry Basics

A **selection of oils** – extra virgin olive oil; vegetable oils (sunflower, peanut, canola) and sesame oil – as well as **red wine vinegar** and **cooking wine**, to add flavour to cooking and make great dressings.

The favourite last-minute **sauces**: ketchup, soy sauce and oyster sauce.

A bottle of **Italian-style tomato sauce** for a tasty and healthy touch in many dishes.

A wide selection of **pasta** (spaghetti, butterfly pasta) and **rice** (basmati, arborio) for quick, inexpensive meals.

Sea salt.

A selection of **spices** to add an exotic touch.

Chicken, vegetable and beef **stock** in whatever form you like it best: powder, cubes or liquid.

Prepared **mustard**, for dressings, for sandwiches.

Canned fish – tuna in oil, sardines and salmon – for satisfying salads and quick, healthy snacks and sandwiches.

Canned fruits and vegetables to help create quick meals and because they're so convenient: baked beans, a selection of vegetables, especially beetroot and tomatoes (diced or whole), a selection of beans (red beans, borlotti), and a selection of canned fruits.

All the **baking essentials**, including: plain flour, self-raising flour and cornflour; a variety of sugars: caster sugar, icing sugar and brown sugar; and cocoa powder.

Semolina and Ham Gnocchi

A satisfying meal, popular with children. It needs to be planned a little in advance.

Serves 4–6

1 litre (2 pints) milk
60 g (2 oz) unsalted butter
1$\frac{1}{4}$ cups semolina
salt to taste
freshly ground black pepper
$\frac{1}{2}$ cup finely chopped ham
$\frac{1}{2}$ cup freshly grated parmesan cheese
2 egg yolks
2 cups Italian-style tomato sauce, bottled or home-made
   (see page 84)

Heat the milk in a large, non-stick pan. When it is almost boiling, add the butter and return to the boil. Whisking vigorously, add the semolina and continue whisking for 3–5 minutes until the mixture thickens.

Add the salt and pepper and cook over a low heat, stirring well with a wooden spoon, for 15 minutes. Remove the pan from the heat. Add the ham and half of the parmesan, then stir well to combine thoroughly. Beat in the egg yolks. Taste and adjust the seasoning.

Spread the mixture in a greased 23 x 33 cm (9 x 14 in) pan. Moisten a spatula with cold water, then pat down the semolina until smooth on top. Allow to cool, then cover with plastic film and chill for at least 2 hours.

Preheat the oven to 220°C (425°F).

Cut the pasta into gnocchi 4 cm (1$\frac{1}{2}$ in) square or use a round cutter. Arrange them in an oiled ovenproof dish and sprinkle with the remaining parmesan. Bake for about 10 minutes until the gnocchi are brown on top.

Meanwhile, heat the tomato sauce. Spoon a little tomato sauce into plates and serve the gnocchi on top.

SAUCES

Some recipes for sauces appear on the next few pages – these sauces are good with pasta but can also be served with potatoes, meat, fish or vegetables. If you're cooking up some pasta, why not have a go at creating your own sauces without following a recipe. Here are a few ideas:

- a little olive oil, freshly ground black pepper and a little freshly grated parmesan cheese
- olive oil, chopped basil or parsley, garlic and parmesan
- chopped sun-dried tomatoes, chopped olives, garlic and chopped parsley
- stir-fried minced beef, pork or chicken with a little curry powder
- canned tuna, olives and chopped parsley
- crumbled ricotta or fetta, olive oil, garlic and chopped parsley
- chopped cooked bacon, pine nuts, chopped parsley and garlic
- olive oil, sautéed chicken livers, garlic and chopped parsley
- scrambled eggs and chopped parsley
- grilled zucchini, eggplant or capsicum, garlic and parmesan
- smoked salmon, olive oil and chopped parsley
- cooked asparagus, a little cream and parmesan
- sautéed spinach, garlic and chilli oil
- cooked beans, such as borlotti, olive oil, garlic and chopped basil or parsley
- anchovies, olives and chopped parsley
- a little mustard, cream and chopped parsley
- blue cheese and chopped parsley
- cooked sliced mushrooms, garlic and herbs
- grilled prosciutto or bacon and parmesan
- roasted or mashed pumpkin, chopped parsley and olive oil

Italian-style Tomato Sauce

This simple, yet delicious, recipe for home-made tomato sauce is great served with pasta, vegetables or fish. The onion, carrot, celery and herbs add aromatic flavours, and the best result is obtained by using a mouli, which makes the texture of the sauce superb.

Makes about 4 cups

about 1½ kg (3 lb) ripe tomatoes
½ medium brown onion
1 stick celery
1 medium-sized carrot, peeled
2 sprigs parsley, basil or thyme
1 clove garlic
freshly ground black pepper
1 tbsp olive oil (optional)

Dice the tomatoes, onion, celery and carrot and place in a saucepan with the herbs, garlic and a little pepper. Cook on medium heat for 20–30 minutes.

Remove the herbs and pass the vegetables through a mouli or fine strainer. Check seasoning and stir in the oil before serving the sauce warm. If you wish, you can add more pepper and freshly chopped herbs such as basil, tarragon or coriander.

Tomato, Bacon and Basil Sauce

This sauce is a good example of how to make a lovely, quick sauce for pasta at home.

Serves 4

2 tbsp olive oil

½ brown onion, chopped

4 slices bacon, cut into small pieces

1 clove garlic, finely chopped

2 tbsp red or white wine (optional)

2 cups Italian-style tomato sauce, bottled or home-made (see page 84)

salt and freshly ground black pepper

3 tbsp chopped basil

2 tbsp freshly grated parmesan cheese

Heat the oil in a saucepan on medium heat. Add the onion and bacon and stir for 3–4 minutes. Add the wine, bring to the boil and boil for 20 seconds. Add the tomato sauce and simmer for 5 minutes.

Season with salt and pepper and, just before serving, stir in garlic, basil and parmesan.

Mushroom and Tomato Sauce

This delicious sauce, which uses either common field mushrooms or wild mushrooms, is perfect for vegetarians when served with pasta, baked potatoes or grilled vegetables.

Serves 4

400 g (14 oz) field or other mushrooms

1 tbsp olive oil

$\frac{1}{2}$ brown onion, chopped

2 tbsp white or red wine

2 cups Italian-style tomato sauce, bottled or home-made (see page 84)

salt and freshly ground black pepper

1 clove garlic, finely chopped

3 tbsp chopped parsley or basil

Briefly wash the mushrooms in a large amount of cold water, then slice.

Heat the oil in a large, non-stick pan or wok. Stir in the onion for 1 minute without browning. Add the mushrooms and cook on a high heat for about 5 minutes. Add the wine and bring to the boil, then add the tomato sauce. Bring to a simmer and cook for 3 minutes. Season to taste with salt and pepper and, just before serving, stir in the garlic and parsley.

Bolognaise Sauce

This pasta sauce is popular with everyone. If you wish, double the quantity and freeze some of it in freezer bags.

Serves 4–6

1 small brown onion

1 medium-sized carrot

1 stick celery

1 tsp olive oil

500 g (1 lb) minced lean meat (pork, beef, veal or a mixture)

1 tbsp plain flour

1 tbsp tomato paste

$1/2$ cup red wine

2 cloves garlic, crushed

400 g (14 oz) can diced or crushed tomatoes

salt and freshly ground black pepper

Peel the onion and carrot. Finely chop the onion, carrot and celery. This can be done in a food processor.

In a saucepan, heat the oil and gently fry the onion, celery and carrot for about 5 minutes. Add the meat and cook on a high heat until the meat has changed colour. Stir in the flour and tomato paste. Add the wine, stir and boil for 10 seconds before stirring in the garlic and tomatoes.

Season with salt and pepper, lower the heat, cover the pan and simmer for 1 hour (or longer, if you wish your sauce to have a richer, sweeter taste).

Singapore Noodles with Shrimps and Pork

This popular noodle dish is a real treat. It is best not to overseason with the curry spices. Spring onion and coriander leaves play an important role in keeping the dish fresh-tasting. You can use chicken instead of pork if you wish.

Serves 3

2 tbsp vegetable oil

2 thin slices ginger

1 clove garlic, finely chopped

1 tsp curry powder

1 cup finely sliced celery

1 medium-sized carrot, peeled, quartered lengthwise and finely sliced

2 tbsp water

about 120 g (4 oz) fresh egg noodles, available from the refrigerated section of supermarkets or Asian grocery shops

100 g ($3^{1}/_{2}$ oz) shrimps

100 g ($3^{1}/_{2}$ oz) roast pork (from Chinese take-away), sliced into bite-sized pieces

1 cup bean sprouts, washed and tailed

1 hard-boiled egg, chopped

3 spring (green) onions, cut into 3 cm (1 in) lengths

1 tbsp soy sauce

$^{1}/_{4}$ cup coriander leaves

Heat a wok. Add the oil and on a high heat stir-fry the ginger, garlic, curry powder, celery and carrot for about 2 minutes. Add the water down the side of the wok and stir-fry for a further 2 minutes.

Meanwhile, place the noodles in a bowl and cover with boiling water. Drain after 3 minutes.

Add the shrimps and pork to the vegetables and stir well for 1 minute. Add the bean sprouts and stir-fry for 30 seconds. Gently add the noodles, egg, spring onion and soy sauce and toss together well. Serve sprinkled with coriander leaves.

Stir-fried Bean Curd with Noodles and Vegetables

Serves 2

Fried bean curd has a firmer texture and is more flavoursome than fresh bean curd. It is an excellent source of protein for vegetarians. You will find bean curd in the refrigerator in most super-markets

4 small bok choy

about 100 g (3$\frac{1}{2}$ oz) fresh thick Asian noodles

1 tbsp vegetable oil

$\frac{1}{2}$ clove garlic, chopped

$\frac{1}{2}$ red chilli, finely sliced

150 g (5 oz) fried bean curd, cut into 1 cm ($\frac{1}{2}$ in) sticks (from supermarket refrigerator)

$\frac{1}{2}$ tbsp fish sauce

1 tbsp soy sauce

1 cup bean sprouts

juice of $\frac{1}{4}$ lemon or $\frac{1}{2}$ small lemon

2 tbsp coriander leaves

Trim off any damaged leaves from the bok choy then quarter the bok choy.

Bring a large pan of water, three-quarters full, to the boil. Add the bok choy, boil for 1 minute, then lift out of the water and drain. Add the noodles to the boiling water and cook for a few minutes until done. Drain the noodles.

Heat the oil in a wok. Add the garlic, chilli and bean curd, and stir-fry gently for 1 minute. Add the cooked bok choy and stir-fry for 2 minutes. Add the fish sauce, soy sauce and bean sprouts and stir-fry for 10 seconds. Add the noodles and stir gently.

Squeeze the lemon juice over and serve sprinkled with coriander leaves.

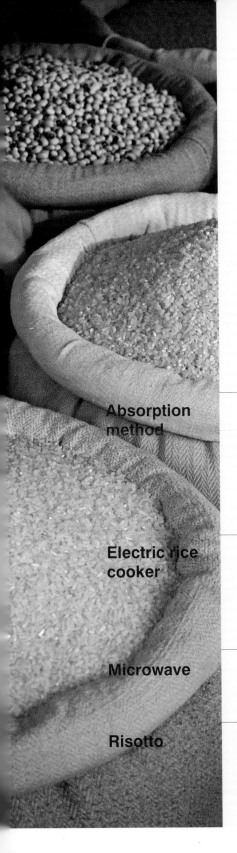

Cooking Rice

Depending on the dish you are cooking, you will need between a quarter and half a cup of uncooked rice per person. In most cases, rice comes washed from the manufacturer. If you want to, you can wash uncooked rice briefly in a bowl of cold water, then drain it. Rice that is to be used in risotto, however, must not be washed as this will affect the final texture of the dish.

Most varieties of rice take between 15 and 22 minutes to cook, using traditional techniques. Most rice varieties are best cooked until tender, but not mushy, and with a little firmness left in the centre of the grain. **Brown rice** is cooked like white rice, except that brown rice takes longer. Allow between 30 and 50 minutes, depending on the variety.

Absorption method

Many rice dishes are cooked by the 'absorption method' where the rice is placed in a saucepan with just the right amount of liquid (water or stock) to cook it. On average, the ratio is $1^1/2$ cups of liquid to one cup of rice. By the time the rice is cooked, the liquid has been absorbed by the rice. Some varieties of rice, such as jasmine and basmati, can be cooked like pasta in a large quantity of boiling water, then drained before serving. For flavour, however, the absorption method is usually preferred.

Electric rice cooker

For big rice eaters, an electric rice cooker makes cooking rice easy. It cooks by the absorption method, but refer to the instructions that come with the cooker. Rice can be cooked successfully in an electric pressure cooker. It's very fast – about 10 minutes from beginning to end for basmati, jasmine or risotto.

Microwave

You can also cook rice in the microwave following your unit's instructions. Remember, a small quantity of rice will take less time than a larger quantity when done in the microwave.

Risotto

Risotto is made by adding small quantities of a simmering liquid to the rice on a low heat. When the rice has absorbed the liquid, more liquid is added. Traditionally, the rice is stirred continously during the cooking of risotto. Less stirring is needed if a non-stick saucepan is used.

Fragrant 'Doongara' Rice

'Doongara' rice is a quality, long-grain Australian variety which cooks easily and provides excellent nutrition. Nutritionists recommend it for those with diabetes or on a weight-loss diet and for athletes, because it has a low glycaemic index. It is available from most supermarkets, usually labelled 'Doongara CleverRice'.

Serves 4

1 tbsp olive oil
$\frac{1}{2}$ brown onion, finely chopped
$\frac{1}{2}$ tsp caraway seeds
$\frac{1}{2}$ tsp turmeric powder
1 tsp sea salt
freshly ground black pepper
1$\frac{1}{4}$ cups 'Doongara' rice
a bit less than 2 cups boiling water

Heat the oil in a non-stick saucepan, then stir in onion and caraway seeds and fry for 2 minutes. Stir in the turmeric powder, salt and pepper. Add the rice and stir well for 1 minute. Add the boiling water, reduce to a low simmer and cover with a close-fitting lid. Cook for about 15 minutes.

Taste the rice to test whether it is cooked. Stir the rice gently and serve.

If you need to cook the rice in advance, you can reheat it in the microwave or the oven.

Nasi Goreng – Indonesian Fried Rice

Every Indonesian family has a different version of this wonderful recipe so you can adapt it to suit your taste or to what's in the fridge! It is best cooked in a wok or large, non-stick frypan and using cold cooked rice.

Serves 2

1 egg

2 tbsp vegetable oil

1 tbsp dried onion flakes

1 small brown onion, chopped

1 clove garlic, chopped

$1/4$ tsp shrimp paste, dissolved in 1 tbsp hot water (optional)

100 g ($3^1/2$ oz) shrimps or 4 prawns, each cut into 3 pieces

200 g (7 oz) lean pork loin or rump steak, cut into small strips

2 cups cold cooked rice

4 spring (green) onions, diced

2 cups cooked peas or other cooked vegetables, diced

1 tbsp light soy sauce

Beat the egg in a small bowl.

Heat half a tablespoon of the oil in the wok. Pour in the beaten egg and make an omelette. Transfer the cooked egg to a plate and, when it is cold, cut it into thin strips.

Heat the remaining oil in the wok and briefly stir-fry the onion flakes. Transfer the onion to the plate.

Add the chopped raw onion and garlic to the wok and stir-fry for 3 or 4 minutes. Stir in the diluted shrimp paste. With the wok on a high heat, add the shrimps and meat and stir until cooked.

Add the rice, spring onions and peas and toss gently until heated through. Stir in the soy sauce, scatter the egg strips and onion flakes on top and serve.

Mussel Risotto

HOW TO CLEAN MUSSELS

Clean the mussels by rubbing them against one another in a container of cold water. Trim the mussels of any beard (hairy bits) or shellfish stuck to the shells.

You can adapt this risotto by adding other pan-fried seafood to it, such as prawns or calamari, just before serving.

Serves 4

1 kg (2 lb) very fresh mussels

$1/4$ cup dry white wine

3 cups cold water

3 sprigs of parsley

1 small brown onion

1 tbsp olive oil

1 large cup arborio rice

2 cups cooked peas

2 tbsp freshly grated parmesan cheese

1 tsp butter

salt and freshly ground black pepper

4 tbsp chopped parsley

Clean the mussels and place them in a large pot. Add the wine, water and parsley sprigs, then cover with a lid and bring to the boil on a high heat. Stir the mussels, using a large spoon. When the shells have opened, transfer them into a bowl, using a slotted spoon. Strain the cooking liquid (mussel stock) through a fine sieve into a saucepan.

Chop the onion finely.

Bring the mussel stock to a low simmer.

Heat the oil in a medium-sized non-stick saucepan and gently fry the onion for about 3 minutes. Add the rice and mix well. Add about 1 cup of the mussel stock, bring to a slow simmer and stir from time to time. When almost all the stock has been absorbed, add another half a cup of stock. Stir and continue to simmer.

Meanwhile, remove the mussels from their shells and discard the shells.

Add more stock to the rice when necessary. The rice will take about 20 minutes to cook.

When the rice is cooked, very gently stir in the cooked peas. Then 1 minute later, add the mussels, parmesan and butter, and season with salt and pepper. Cover with a lid and leave to rest for about 5 minutes.

Serve sprinkled with chopped parsley.

Threshold for Flavours

When the same dish is served to several people, each one appreciates it differently. For some, the dish is perfect, for others it's not salty enough or it's too spicy, and so on. The threshold for salt, sweetness, spiciness, heat and bitterness and everything in between varies from one person to another. Our taste buds are like our fingerprints – everyone has a different set. However, it's good to remember that excess salt, sugar, hot or acidic food can affect our health as we age. So in the interests of good health, it's a good idea to help children acquire healthy eating habits as early as possible. Our own threshold may be unique, but it's also influenced by family habits, ethnic background and peer pressure.

Stir-fried Rice with Peas, Bean Shoots and Bacon

Stir-fried rice is made using cold cooked rice. Asian families use rice leftover from the previous day, adding vegetables, spices and meat or fish to transform it into a delicious meal.

Serves 2

about 100 g ($3^1/2$ oz) bean shoots
1 tbsp vegetable oil
$^1/2$ small brown onion, chopped
2 lean slices bacon, diced
$^1/4$ tsp curry powder
2 cups cold cooked rice
1 cup cooked peas
1 tbsp soy sauce
$^1/2$ tsp chilli paste
a handful of coriander leaves

Wash the bean shoots and pick out any damaged ones.

Heat the oil in a wok or large, non-stick frypan. Add the onion and bacon and stir-fry gently for about 3 minutes or until the onion is transparent and just starting to brown around the edges.

Stir in the curry powder, then add the rice, peas and bean shoots, tossing on high heat until the rice is reheated. Stir in soy sauce and chilli paste, and serve sprinkled with coriander leaves.

Basmati is the rice nutritionists prefer (it is excellent for those with diabetes or on a weight-loss diet) and it's a great rice to serve with Indian food. Jasmine rice and short-grain and medium-grain rice are favoured in Asian dishes as the cooked grains remain moist and cling together, making it easier to eat with chopsticks.

Lemon and Parsley Risotto

This is a simple, delicious dish. I often recommend my students make it the first time they try a risotto. It's much easier to make a risotto in a non-stick saucepan, as you don't need to stir the rice as much during the cooking.

Serves 3

$^1/_2$ brown onion

1 lemon

3 cups chicken stock (see page 40)

1 tbsp olive oil

1 cup arborio rice

$^1/_4$ cup dry white wine

$^1/_2$ tbsp butter

3 tbsp finely grated parmesan cheese

salt and freshly ground black pepper

1 cup finely chopped flat parsley leaves

Peel and finely chop the onion. Grate about 1 tablespoon of the skin (zest) of the lemon, then juice the lemon.

Bring the chicken stock to a simmer in a medium-sized saucepan.

Heat the oil in a non-stick saucepan on a medium heat. Add the chopped onion and stir-fry for about 2 minutes without browning it. Stir in the rice and grated lemon zest, stirring for about 20 seconds. Add the wine, then add about 1 cup of stock. Stir well, bring to a slow simmer and cook until almost all the stock has been absorbed, then add another half cup of stock.

Continue adding stock in small quantities as soon as it has been absorbed each time, stirring occasionally to prevent the rice from sticking and to allow it to cook evenly. It takes about 20 minutes to cook, but taste a few grains of rice to check the cooking. If you run out of stock before the rice is cooked, add a little boiling water.

As soon as the rice is cooked, turn off the heat and gently stir in the butter, parmesan and lemon juice and season with salt and pepper. Cover with a lid and rest for 2 minutes.

Stir in the chopped parsley and serve.

Vegetarian Risotto

I like to start this risotto with chopped onion, carrot and celery, as they provide a good balance of flavour. The main flavour comes from the mushrooms, but you can use other vegetables, such as asparagus, broccoli or peas.

Serves 4

3 cups vegetable stock (see page 41)
200 g (7 oz) button mushrooms
1 small onion
1 medium carrot
1 stick celery
1 tbsp olive oil
1 cup arborio rice
2 tbsp freshly grated parmesan cheese
1 tsp butter
salt and freshly ground black pepper
3 tbsp chopped parsley

Bring the stock to a simmer in a medium-sized saucepan.

Wash and quarter the mushrooms. Add the mushrooms to the stock and simmer them for about 5 minutes. Transfer the mushrooms to a bowl, using a slotted spoon.

Chop the onion, carrot and celery. (This can be done in a blender.)

Heat the oil in a medium-sized non-stick saucepan. Add the chopped vegetables and fry gently for about 3 minutes. Add the rice and mix well. Add about 1 cup of the simmering stock, bring to a slow simmer and stir from time to time. When almost all the stock has been absorbed, add another half cup of stock, stir and continue to simmer. Add more stock when necessary and cook for about 20 minutes or until the rice is almost done.

Stir in the mushrooms, parmesan and butter and season with salt and pepper. Cover the pan, turn off the heat and leave to rest for about 5 minutes. Stir in the chopped parsley and serve.

Chicken Risotto

I make this dish when I have leftover poached or roast chicken. The chicken must not be too dry.

Serves 2

a little more than 1½ cups chicken stock (see page 40)
4 mushrooms
½ brown onion
10 cm (4 in) piece celery
½ tbsp olive oil
a little more than ½ cup arborio rice
about 1 cup cooked chicken, diced
salt and freshly ground black pepper
2 tbsp freshly grated parmesan cheese
1 tsp butter or margarine (optional)
2 tbsp chopped parsley

Bring the stock to a low simmer.

Slice the mushrooms and finely chop the onion and celery.

Heat the oil in a medium-sized non-stick pan. Add the onion and celery and fry gently on a medium heat for 3 minutes. Add the rice and mushrooms and stir for 1 minute. Add about half a cup of chicken stock and bring to a gentle simmer, stirring from time to time. Simmer until almost all the stock has been absorbed, then add another third of a cup of simmering stock.

Continue stirring occasionally and add more stock as needed. It takes about 20 minutes to cook a risotto, but taste a few grains of rice to check the cooking. It's cooked when the grains of rice are soft, except for the centre, which must remain a little firm. If the centre is too hard, it needs more cooking. You may have some stock left over. If you don't have enough stock, add a little boiling water.

When the rice is almost cooked, gently mix in the diced chicken, season with salt and pepper and cook for a further 2 minutes.

Add the parmesan and butter and stir gently. Cover with a lid, turn off the heat and leave to rest for 5 minutes before stirring in the parsley and serving.

How to Take Care of Your Heart

Eat plenty of vegetables of different sorts.

Buy lean minced meat, and remember that sausages, salami and smallgoods contain high levels of fat.

Trim meat of all fat.

Use fat in moderation when you cook.

Cook with polyunsaturated or monounsaturated oils, such as sunflower, safflower, canola or olive oil. Use butter only for special occasions and avoid it if you have a cholesterol problem.

Choose reduced-fat varieties of dairy products such as yoghurt and milk.

Enjoy several fish meals every week. Mackerel, herrings, tuna, sardines and salmon are particularly good fish for the heart.

Avoid deep-frying food and eating deep-fried foods.

Pan-fry in non-stick pans using a minimum of fat.

Visit your doctor to find out whether you have high cholesterol or high blood pressure.

Enjoy high-fibre cereals for breakfast, choosing low-fat milk or soy milk.

Avoid becoming overweight.

Exercise daily to keep fit.

Avoid stressful situations.

Avoid rich snacks. Pastries, biscuits and cakes are often high in fat and sugar.

Choose foods low in salt and avoid adding salt to your meals.

Dietitians and nutritionists are the professionals to consult about choosing the right diet if you have a problem.

Look after your diet if you are a diabetic (see page 51).

Avoid smoking.

Drink acohol in moderation.

MAIN RISK FACTORS FOR YOUR HEART
- Being overweight
- High blood cholesterol
- Physical inactivity
- Smoking
- High blood pressure
- Diabetes Type 2

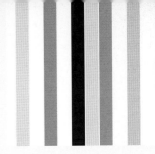

SALADS

When I was little, my grandmother and mother often asked me to help with the preparation of the salad, by washing the tomatoes, peeling the cucumber or drying the salad leaves in the salad spinner. Salads are a great option for the less confident cook, as there is usually very little cooking to do. Become confident by preparing salads, and then improve your cooking skills with other types of dishes.

Cool Summer Salad

Serve this refreshing salad on a hot day when cold food is more appealing.

Serves 3

6 new baby potatoes
100 g (3¹⁄₂ oz) snow peas
1 medium-sized carrot
10 cm (4 in) piece cucumber
1 tomato
¹⁄₂ red capsicum
2 tbsp low-fat natural yoghurt
¹⁄₂ tsp ground sweet paprika
¹⁄₂ tbsp red wine vinegar
salt and freshly ground black pepper

Cook the potatoes in salted boiling water. Drain, cover with cold water and allow to cool.

Top and tail the snow peas and place in a bowl. Cover with boiling water and stand for 5 minutes. Drain and cool in cold water, then drain again.

Peel the carrot and cucumber, then cut into thin sticks. Dice the tomato. Slice the capsicum very thinly.

Mix the yoghurt in the salad bowl with the paprika and vinegar.

Add the potatoes to the bowl with the snow peas, carrot, tomato, cucumber and capsicum and season with salt and pepper. Toss the salad to coat with the yoghurt dressing and serve.

Egg and Celeriac Salad

At home in France during my youth, grated celeriac was as popular as grated carrots. Celeriac is a winter root vegetable which is very firm. Chose regular-shaped and unblemished celeriac. Small celeriac are preferable to medium-sized as they are sweeter.

Serves 4

1 egg yolk
1 tsp prepared hot mustard
1 tsp vinegar
salt and freshly ground black pepper
3 tbsp oil, e.g. peanut, canola
about 500 g (1 lb) celeriac
2 tomatoes, diced
the heart of a butter lettuce, about 8 leaves
2 hard-boiled eggs
2 tbsp finely cut chives or parsley

In a large bowl place the egg yolk, mustard, vinegar and a little salt and pepper and whisk until very smooth. Slowly pour in the oil, whisking continuously to make a thick sauce.

Peel and grate the celeriac. Add the celeriac to the sauce with the diced tomatoes and stir well.

Wash the lettuce leaves, arrange on plates and top with the celeriac salad.

Peel and chop the hard-boiled eggs. Scatter the egg over the top of the salad, sprinkle with chives or parsley and serve.

Four-bean and Beetroot Salad

If you are cooking the beetroot yourself, select beetroot of a similar size, preferably small. Wash well and cook in salted water in the same way you would cook carrots. It will take from 20 minutes to 1 hour, depending on the size of the beetroot.

For this easy, nourishing salad, select a variety of canned beans of your choice from the supermarket, health food shop or deli.

Serves 3–4

juice of 1 lemon

1 clove garlic, finely chopped

salt and freshly ground black pepper

2 tbsp extra virgin olive oil or 2 tbsp natural yoghurt

4 canned baby beetroot (or freshly cooked)

400 g (14 oz) can Four Bean Mix, drained

2 tomatoes, diced

1/2 small red onion, diced

2 tbsp parsley

In a salad bowl, mix the lemon juice with the garlic, a little salt and pepper and the oil.

Peel the beetroot if you are using fresh ones. Dice the beetroot and place it in a salad bowl with the dressing. Add the drained beans, tomato, onion and parsley. Toss gently and serve with a wholegrain bread.

Beetroot and Walnut Salad

This salad uses cooked beetroot and is very simple to prepare. Here I use a yoghurt dressing, but you can make a normal vinaigrette, using either lemon or vinegar with oil, and add plenty of parsley, chives or mint.

Serves 2

2 tbsp low-fat yoghurt

juice of $1/4$ lemon

freshly ground black pepper

6 cooked baby beetroot or enough cooked beetroot for 2

2 tbsp walnut flesh

about 1 tbsp chopped parsley

Combine the yoghurt, lemon juice and a little black pepper in a bowl.

Cut the beetroot into quarters or cubes or slice them. Add the beetroot to the yoghurt and stir in the walnuts and chopped parsley.

French Cucumber and Tomato Salad with Sour Cream Dressing

Enjoy this salad on a hot summer's day with barbecued or grilled fish or cold meat. The cucumber is peeled, then cut into long thin strips, using a peeler.

Serves 2–3

1 continental (telegraph) cucumber
1/2 tbsp sea salt, which is later washed off
2 tbsp light sour cream
freshly ground black pepper
1 tsp red wine vinegar
2 medium-sized tomatoes
2 tbsp chopped parsley, chives or dill

Peel the cucumber. Cut the flesh into long, thin strips, using a peeler – once you reach the seeds, discard the centre. Place the cucumber strips with the salt in a bowl and mix well. Cover with plastic wrap and refrigerate for at least 30 minutes.

During that time, some of the cucumber's water content will be expelled. Strain the cucumber, discarding the juice, then rinse the cucumber briefly under cold water. Squeeze out the liquid and place the cucumber in a bowl with the sour cream, a little pepper and the vinegar. Toss well.

Remove the cores of the tomatoes, then slice the tomatoes thinly.

Arrange the tomato slices on a serving dish, spoon the cucumber on top, sprinkle with parsley and serve.

Grated Carrot
and Celeriac Salad

This refreshing salad is full of goodness and is perfect to serve at a barbecue instead of coleslaw. It goes well with grilled fish. Use finely shredded cabbage leaves if celeriac is unavailable.

Serves 4

2 medium-sized carrots

about $\frac{1}{4}$ medium-sized celeriac

1–2 tsp prepared mustard

2 tsp red wine vinegar

$\frac{1}{4}$ tsp curry powder

salt and freshly ground black pepper

$\frac{1}{2}$ cup Greek-style or other yoghurt

2 tbsp sultanas

2 tbsp finely cut chives or other herb

Peel and wash the carrots and celeriac, then grate them coarsely.

In a salad bowl, mix the mustard, vinegar, curry powder and a little salt and pepper with the yoghurt. Add the grated vegetables and mix well.

Add the sultanas, sprinkle with finely cut chives and serve.

New Potato, Tomato and Rocket Salad

Choose small, regular-shaped potatoes, the best-smelling, sweet tomatoes and the most tender-looking rocket. This salad is great served with leftover meat or fish.

Serves 2

6–8 new baby potatoes
salt
1 tsp red wine vinegar
freshly ground black pepper
1 tbsp olive oil
$\frac{1}{2}$ clove garlic, finely chopped
2 medium-sized tomatoes
1 small carrot, peeled and grated
a handful of rocket
2 tbsp finely chopped chives or other herb
1 egg, hard-boiled and quartered
$\frac{1}{4}$ red onion, cut into rings

Place the potatoes unpeeled in a saucepan, cover with cold water and add some salt. Bring to the boil and cook for 10–15 minutes or until tender. Drain the potatoes and cool in cold water. Peel and halve the potatoes.

In a salad bowl, mix the vinegar with a little salt and pepper, the olive oil and the garlic. Add the halved potatoes, the tomatoes, each cut into about twelve segments, the grated carrot, rocket, egg, onion rings and chives.

Toss well just before serving.

Gruyère, Apple and Celery Salad

In this light 'bachelor' meal you can also include some salad greens or other vegetables, such as capsicum, avocado or beetroot.

Serves 1

2 sticks celery
1 small to medium-sized carrot
30 g (1 oz) Gruyère or other cheese
1 tbsp chopped walnut
1 tbsp yoghurt
juice of ¼ lemon
a pinch of curry powder
a little salt and freshly ground black pepper
1 large apple, e.g. Granny Smith or Golden Delicious

If necessary, peel the stringy side of the celery. Wash the celery, cut it into thin slices and place in a bowl. Peel and grate the carrot and add it to the bowl.

Cut the Gruyère into matchsticks and add to the bowl. Mix in the walnut, yoghurt, lemon juice, curry powder and a little salt and pepper.

Peel, quarter and core the apple and slice it thinly. Add the apple to the salad and mix well. Refrigerate or serve immediately.

Mixed Salad for a Barbecue

Here's a substantial mixed salad to serve at a barbecue instead of
serving several different salads.

Serves 8

8 small potatoes
salt
500 g (1 lb) young green beans
1 tsp Dijon mustard
1 tbsp red wine vinegar
juice of 1 lemon
freshly ground black pepper
4 tbsp olive oil
8 small tomatoes
$^1/_2$ red onion, diced or thinly sliced
about 30 black olives
4 hard-boiled eggs, shelled

Wash the potatoes. Place them whole in a saucepan, cover with
cold water and add a little salt. Bring to the boil and cook the
potatoes for 10–15 minutes or until just soft. Drain and place in
cold water to cool. Drain when cold.

Top and tail the beans and cook in salted boiling water for
5–8 minutes or until just tender. Drain the beans and place in
ice-cold water to cool. Drain when cold.

In a large salad bowl, whisk the mustard with the vinegar, lemon
juice and a little salt and pepper. Whisk in the olive oil.

Wash, core and quarter the tomatoes and add to the bowl.

Peel and slice the potatoes and add to the bowl. Add the beans,
olives and onion and toss gently.

Garnish the top of the salad with quarters of hard-boiled egg.
Serve with grilled meat or fish.

Salad of Mixed Bitter Leaves

**HOW TO WASH
SALAD GREENS**

Discard any
damaged leaves
before gently
washing the
leaves in a large
amount of water.
Lift the leaves
from the water
into a colander
(or salad spin-
ner) and drain.

Both supermarkets and greengrocers stock a superb variety of
colourful salad leaves. For a special touch add walnut pieces or
diced cheese.

Serves 4

about 150 g (5 oz) rocket or mesclun

1 small radicchio

2 small yellow witlof (Belgian endive)

1 small clove garlic, finely chopped (optional)

salt and freshly ground black pepper

1 tbsp red wine vinegar

2½ tbsp extra virgin olive oil

Trim or discard any damaged salad leaves. Carefully pull off the
leaves of the radicchio and the witlof. Gently wash all the leaves
in a large amount of cold water. Drain and shake the leaves to
remove excess water or use a salad spinner.

In a large salad bowl, combine the garlic, a little salt and pepper
and the vinegar. Slowly whisk in the oil.

Toss the leaves in the dressing and serve.

Gado-Gado (Indonesian Salad)

A great Asian salad that makes a satisfying light meal in summer.

Serves about 6

4 small potatoes

200 g (7 oz) small green beans, topped and tailed

100 g (3$\frac{1}{2}$ oz) bean sprouts

1 medium-sized carrot, peeled and cut into long, fine strips

$\frac{1}{2}$ red capsicum, halved and cut into long, thin strips

1 cup finely shredded cabbage

salt and freshly ground black pepper

juice of 1 lemon

3 hard-boiled eggs, peeled and quartered

1$\frac{1}{2}$ cups satay sauce, bottled or home-made
(see Peanut Sauce, page 169)

Boil the potatoes in their skins. When done, cool in cold water. Peel and slice the potatoes.

Cook the beans in boiling water until just done. Cool in cold water, then drain.

Place the bean sprouts in a bowl and cover with boiling water. Drain after 20 seconds, then cool in cold water. Drain again.

In a large salad bowl, mix the beans, carrot, capsicum, bean sprouts and cabbage. Season with salt, pepper and lemon juice. Top with the sliced potatoes and quartered eggs.

Spoon the satay sauce over the salad or serve separately.

After-Christmas Turkey and Mango Salad

Cold food, such as salad, tastes more flavoursome when it is served at room temperature rather than chilled, straight from the refrigerator. Remove pre-prepared food from the fridge 10–15 minutes before serving.

Salads are perfect for using up leftovers. You can use ham, roast pork or chicken instead of turkey in this salad, and substitute peaches or apricots for the mango if you like.

Serves 2

3 tbsp plain yoghurt

juice of $\frac{1}{2}$ lemon or $\frac{1}{2}$ tbsp red wine vinegar

a large pinch of curry powder

salt and freshly ground black pepper

2 cups turkey meat, thinly sliced or cubed

1 tbsp finely chopped walnuts

$\frac{1}{2}$ ripe mango, diced

1 cup cooked beans, cut into small pieces, or 1 cup salad leaves

$\frac{1}{2}$ cup grated carrot (optional)

2 tbsp chives, cut into 5 mm ($\frac{1}{4}$ in) pieces, or other herb

In a salad bowl, mix the yoghurt with the lemon juice, curry powder and a little salt and pepper.

Add the turkey meat, walnuts, mango, beans, grated carrot and chives. Toss well and serve immediately or refrigerate until 10 minutes before serving.

Pineapple, Pecan, Date and Rice Salad

This salad was inspired by a visit to Coffs Harbour on the northern coast of New Sould Wales, where pecans and pineapple are farmed. Try this for a light brunch.

Serves 3–4

1/2 cup skim-milk yoghurt

1 cup diced pineapple, fresh or canned

1/2 tsp curry powder (optional)

salt and freshly ground black pepper

2 cups cooked rice

1/2 cup pecan nuts, chopped

1 cup grated carrot

1 cup diced celery

6 dates, pitted and each cut into 4 pieces

4 spring (green) onions, finely cut

In a large bowl, combine the yoghurt, pineapple, curry powder and a little salt and pepper.

Add the cooked rice, pecan nuts, grated carrot, diced celery, dates and spring onions. Toss well and serve straight away or refrigerate until about 10 minutes before serving.

Roast Chicken, Green Bean and Cashew Salad

Select a good-quality roast chicken if you are buying it ready-cooked and make sure the mango is perfectly ripe for this delicious summer salad.

Serves 4–6

juice of 1 lemon
½ tsp curry powder
salt and freshly ground black pepper
4 tbsp Greek-style yoghurt
1 cold roast chicken, about size 14
250 g (8 oz) cold, cooked green beans
1 ripe mango
2 butter lettuce leaves per person, washed
2 tbsp cashew nuts (raw or roasted)
3 spring (green) onions, finely sliced

Place the lemon juice in a small bowl. Stir in the curry powder and a little salt and pepper, then mix in the yoghurt.

Detach the meat from the bones of the chicken, cut it into bite-sized pieces and place in the bowl.

Cut the beans into bite-sized pieces.

Peel the mango and cut the flesh into small, bite-sized pieces.

Place the lettuce leaves on a serving plate and top with the beans, mango, chicken, cashew nuts and spring onion. Spoon the yoghurt dressing over the salad and serve.

Marinated John Dory Salad

The fish used here is cured rather than cooked. Over several hours the acid in the marinade (in this case, the lime juice) turns the raw fish opaque white and cures it. It's perfectly safe to eat, and it's delicious!

John Dory is a delicious, white fish with delicate flesh. You could also use blue eye, barramundi or flathead.

Serves 2

250 g (8 oz) very fresh John Dory fillets, skinned and boneless

juice of 1 lime

3 drops tabasco

$^1/_4$ tsp cracked pepper

1 tbsp olive oil or vegetable oil

1 large tomato, diced

$^1/_2$ green capsicum, diced

$^1/_2$ cup peeled, seeded, diced cucumber

juice of $^1/_2$ lemon

salt

1 tbsp finely cut chives

Cut the fish into strips about 6 cm (2$^1/_2$ in) long and 1 cm ($^1/_2$ in) thick. Place the fish in a bowl with the lime juice, tabasco, cracked pepper and half the oil and toss gently. Cover with plastic film and refrigerate for about 4 hours.

Place the tomato, capsicum and cucumber in a bowl. Season with the remaining oil, the lemon juice and a little salt. Toss well and put aside for about half an hour before serving.

Spoon a little salad onto each plate. Top with the drained fish, sprinkle with chives and serve.

Red Salmon Salad

Here we use canned salmon. As a variation, prepare this
satisfying salad using other types of fish, such as tuna, sardines or
mackerel.

Serves 2

200 g (7 oz) baby green beans, as small as possible

$\frac{1}{2}$ red capsicum, seeds removed

about 1 tbsp chopped white or red onion

2 tbsp chopped parsley

salt and freshly ground black pepper

$\frac{1}{2}$ tbsp red wine vinegar

1 tsp prepared Dijon or hot mustard

$1\frac{1}{2}$ tbsp olive oil

200 g (7 oz) can red salmon, drained

1 hard-boiled egg, quartered (optional)

Top and tail the beans, then cook them in salted boiling water for
about 5 minutes or until they are just done. Drain and place them
in very cold water to halt the cooking. Then drain them again.

Cut the capsicum into very thin strips, then place it in a bowl
with the beans, onion and parsley.

In a small bowl whisk together a little salt, pepper, vinegar and
mustard. Slowly whisk in the oil.

Gently toss the vegetables in the dressing and arrange them on
plates. Top each serve with drained salmon. Garnish with
quarters of egg and serve.

Cold Roast Meat with a Rocket and Roast Vegetable Salad

This is an easy way to use leftover roast meat and vegetables. Use beef, lamb, pork or chicken, slice the meat very thinly and trim off any fat and skin.

Serves 2

2 pieces cold roast potato

2 pieces cold roast pumpkin

2 pieces cold roast carrot

1 tsp prepared hot English mustard

$\frac{1}{2}$ tbsp red wine vinegar

salt and freshly ground black pepper

1$\frac{1}{2}$ tbsp olive oil

about 1 cup rocket leaves

1 tbsp diced red onion

2 tbsp finely sliced parsley or coriander leaves

enough sliced cold roast meat for 2 people

1 tbsp diced gherkins (optional)

Cut the potato, pumpkin and carrot into slices 1 cm ($\frac{1}{2}$ in) thick.

In a small bowl combine the mustard, vinegar, a little salt, pepper and the oil.

Arrange the rocket leaves on two plates. Top with the vegetables and sprinkle with the onion and parsley or coriander leaves. Lay the thin slices of cold meat on top and scatter the gherkin over them. Drizzle the dressing over the salad and serve.

Roast Beef Salad
with a Basil Dressing

Cold roast beef is delicious in a sandwich, but in a salad it can provide an even more enjoyable meal. Trim the meat of all visible fat and slice it very finely just before mixing the salad.

Serves 2

8 small new potatoes

a handful of green salad leaves

1 large tomato

about 12 basil leaves

$^1/_2$ tsp red wine vinegar

$^1/_2$ clove garlic, very finely chopped

$1^1/_2$ tbsp olive oil

salt and freshly ground black pepper

6 raw almonds, finely chopped (optional)

6–8 very thinly cut slices of roast beef

Place the unpeeled potatoes in a saucepan and cover with salted water. Boil for 10–15 minutes or until cooked. Drain and cool in cold water. Drain again and peel.

Wash and spin or pat dry the salad leaves. Wash and dice the tomato, removing its core.

Chop the basil finely and mix in a salad bowl with the vinegar, garlic, oil, a little salt and pepper and the chopped almonds.

Cut the beef into bite-sized pieces and place in the bowl, together with the peeled potatoes, salad leaves and diced tomato. Toss well and serve.

Spring Lamb Salad with Tahini Dressing

Almost any cut of lamb will do for this dish which is a meal in itself. If using leftover meat, say from a roast leg, a mini roast or the shoulder, slice it very thinly to ensure that it is tender and easy to eat.

Serves 2

200 g (7 oz) green beans
a handful of green leaves, e.g. butter lettuce, rocket
1/4 red onion, finely sliced
2 artichoke hearts, preserved in oil, drained and quartered
8 cherry tomatoes, halved
2 tbsp coriander leaves, finely sliced
1 tbsp olive oil
1/2 tbsp tahini (sesame seed paste)
juice of 1 lemon
1/2 clove garlic, finely chopped
1/2 tbsp cold water
salt and freshly ground black pepper
about 200 g (7 oz) lean, cold leftover roast lamb, very thinly sliced

Top and tail the beans then cook them in a saucepan of salted boiling water for about 5 minutes. Drain and cool the beans in cold water, then drain again.

Wash and dry the salad leaves.

Place the beans in a bowl with the onion, quartered artichokes, halved cherry tomatoes, green leaves and coriander.

In a small bowl, whisk the olive oil with the tahini, lemon juice and garlic, then whisk in the water little by little until it is runny like a dressing. Season with salt and pepper.

Add two-thirds of the dressing to the salad and toss gently. Spoon the salad onto plates and top with slices of cold lamb. Drizzle the remaining dressing over the lamb and serve.

DRESSINGS

A dressing enhances other food by adding flavour and moisture. I say 'food' because nowadays dressings are not restricted to salads but are used as an alternative to butter on grilled fish, meat and vegetables and also on some steamed and boiled vegetables.

Most dressings combine oil of some sort with acidity in the form of lemon juice or vinegar. The rule of thumb is to use three times the quantity of oil to vinegar or lemon, for example, three tablespoons of olive oil to one tablespoon of vinegar.

Dressings are usually seasoned with a little salt and pepper, while chopped herbs such as parsley, basil or oregano can give a distinctive touch. Oregano provides a Greek touch, basil or tarragon a more Italian or French flavour. Adding chopped onion, shallots or garlic gives the dressing character or a little bite.

Other ingredients such as nuts (for example, almonds or cashews) or chopped vegetables (such as capsicum, tomato and cucumber) enhance the texture. Such dressings are sometimes referred to as salsas.

Vinegars

On an everyday basis, I use a flavoursome red wine vinegar in many dressings. I like sherry vinegar or raspberry vinegar for a special touch in a dish. For special occasions, I use a more expensive balsamic vinegar which has an intense, beautiful flavour.

Balsamic vinegar is an intense red wine vinegar traditionally made in Modena in the north of Italy. It is superb used in small quantities in dressings with olive or any other type of oil. Many large manufacturers make affordable commercial balsamic vinegar but it's worthwhile paying a little more to get the real artisanal product which has more depth and flavour.

Oils

Choose which oil to use for your dressing according to what flavour you want in the particular dish. Extra virgin olive oil has a strong, fruity flavour and is perfect with most Mediterranean-style salads. For Asian dressings, I use a vegetable oil, such as peanut or macadamia oil, and I reserve those like walnut, sesame and hazelnut oil, for special salads in which I want the flavour of the oil to dominate. All oils have similar high fat levels. Coconut oil and palm oil contain cholesterol.

Olive oils are classified in order to help consumers understand their qualities. **Extra virgin olive oil** is obtained from the first pressing of the olives, done solely under mechanical or physical pressure, and the olives are not heated. To obtain the classification of 'extra virgin', the oil needs to have a level of acidity lower than one per cent, which is desirable for the flavour. Extra virgin olive oil has a green tinge and a strong flavour. All countries producing olives make extra virgin olive oil. **Virgin olive oil** is made in the same way as extra virgin olive oil, but its acidity level is higher than one per cent, and it is therefore considered less fine.

Balsamic and Olive Oil Dressing

Dressings may vary from one Mediterranean country to another, but good olive oil remains the common ingredient. The acidity is provided by either vinegar or lemon juice, and various condiments such as pepper, garlic, onions or herbs are added for extra zest. Getting the balance of oil and vinegar just right is a question of taste and experience.

Serves about 4

about 1 tbsp balsamic vinegar

salt and a little freshly ground black pepper

about 3 tbsp olive oil

1 clove garlic, finely chopped

1 tbsp chopped parsley, basil or other herb

In a small bowl thoroughly mix the vinegar, salt and pepper, then mix in the olive oil, garlic and herbs. Taste and add more vinegar or oil to balance the flavour.

If you have to prepare the dressing well in advance, add the chopped garlic and herbs just before serving.

A Lighter Mayonnaise

If the oil and yolk separate, do the following: Place an egg yolk in a clean bowl. Add a teaspoon of vinegar and a teaspoon of prepared mustard and whisk well. While continuing to whisk, very slowly pour the separated mayonnaise over the egg yolk preparation. It will come together well if you are patient enough.

With plenty of flavour, this mayonnaise contains about 25% less fat than a standard version. However, it is still rich when compared to a dressing made with yoghurt and lemon juice.

Serves 4–6

1 egg yolk

1 tsp prepared hot mustard

1 tsp red wine vinegar

4 tbsp vegetable oil

2 tbsp light sour cream

freshly ground black pepper

salt (optional)

Whisk or (using an electric beater) beat the egg yolk, mustard and vinegar for 10 seconds. While continuing to beat, slowly add the oil. When they are well combined, whisk in the sour cream and season with pepper and salt.

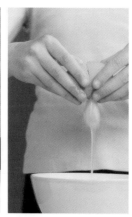
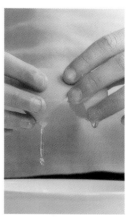

Make-believe Mayonnaise

This cold sauce resembles a mayonnaise in both appearance and flavour and is made using soft cheese with a very low fat content. The result is not cheesy and the smooth sauce contains less than a third of the calories of traditional mayonnaise made with oil.

Serves about 6

about 150 g (5 oz) low-fat soft cheese, e.g. quark or a smooth, low-fat cottage cheese
2 eggs
2 tsp prepared hot English mustard
3 tbsp low-fat milk
salt and freshly ground black pepper

Remove the cheese from the refrigerator to bring it to room temperature.

Bring a small pan of water to the boil and cook the eggs for 7–8 minutes. Remove the eggs and refresh them in cold water for about 10 seconds before peeling them while still warm. Halve the eggs, scoop out the warm yolks and place the yolks in an electric blender. (Keep the whites for another use.) Add the mustard, milk, soft cheese, salt and a little freshly ground pepper. Blend to a smooth, creamy consistency. Place in a serving bowl, or in the refrigerator if you do not plan to use it within an hour.

Serve with salads, cold meats, fish or vegetables.

Olive Oil Dressing with Tomato and Dill

A dressing to serve with warm vegetables, such as beans or zucchini, or with poached or grilled fish. If you wish, you can also warm the dressing a little, and the dill can be replaced by another herb.

Serves about 4

1 large tomato or 2 small ones
salt and freshly ground black pepper
1 tbsp red wine vinegar
3 tbsp olive oil
1 clove garlic, finely chopped (optional)
1/2 white onion or 1 shallot, finely chopped
2 tbsp finely cut dill

Cut out the eye of the tomato, place the tomato in a bowl and cover with boiling water. After 15 seconds, remove the tomato from the bowl and dip it in cold water. Peel and halve the tomato, then gently squeeze out and discard the seeds and cut the flesh into small dice.

In a mixing bowl, combine a little salt and pepper with the vinegar. Then add the tomato, oil, garlic, onion and dill, and serve.

Peeling and Roasting Nuts

To peel **almonds** and **pistachio nuts**, place them in boiling water for 30 seconds then drain. Put the nuts on kitchen paper or a clean tea towel and peel quickly before they cool.

Hazelnuts are peeled and roasted by placing them under a hot grill and moving them around to make sure they don't burn. Keep an eye on them and when the skin has cracked, place them in a tea towel and rub together to loosen the skin.

Almonds and **pine nuts** are roasted in a very hot oven for about 10 minutes. Stir them around frequently. Alternatively, roast almonds in a frying pan or wok in a teaspoon of oil, stirring constantly.

Hazelnut and Chive Dressing

Truly a special dressing to serve with vegetables such as
asparagus, artichokes or tomatoes, with grilled vegetables, grilled
chicken or fish, or simply with a salad of tender, green leaves.

Serves 2–3

6 hazelnuts, roasted or raw, with or without skins
1/2 tbsp red wine vinegar or juice of 1/2 lemon
salt and freshly ground black pepper
2 tbsp olive oil
1 tbsp finely cut chives

Chop the hazelnuts into small pieces.

Mix the vinegar with a little salt and pepper in a bowl. Add the
oil, then gently stir in the hazelnuts and chives.

Soy Sauce Salad Dressing

This Asian-flavoured dressing goes well with hot or cold steamed
vegetables, such as asparagus, cabbage, Chinese broccoli and
zucchini. It's also delicious served on baked or grilled fish and
chicken.

Serves 4

juice of 1/2 lemon or 2 tsp red wine vinegar
1 tsp sesame oil
a little freshly ground black pepper
1 tbsp light soy sauce
2 tbsp vegetable oil
1/2 red chilli, seeded and finely sliced (optional)
1/2 clove garlic, finely chopped
1 tbsp sesame seeds (optional)

In a bowl, combine the lemon juice, sesame oil, pepper, soy
sauce, vegetable oil and chilli.

Just before dressing the food, add the garlic and sesame seeds.

VEGETABLE DISHES

Every major health organisation reports that most of us don't eat enough vegetables. Yet it's really worthwhile making an effort in this department in order to reduce the risk of heart disease, certain cancers, diabetes and other illnesses. Learn to cook as many vegetables as you can in lots of different ways, and vary the selection too. Learn to season vegetables with fresh herbs, spices, lemon juice, ginger, garlic, olive oil and other interesting condiments that are low in salt, sugar and fat. And learn to cook a range of vegetarian dishes – you'll find some in this section and also in the sections on soups, salads, snacks and pasta and rice. If you are a vegetarian, make sure you understand how to nourish yourself properly. There are many books on the subject and you can obtain information on the internet.

Modern Mixed Green Vegetables

Lovers of green vegetables will enjoy this special mix which can be served with grilled fish or poultry.

Serves 2

3 baby bok choy
150 g (5 oz) young beans
6 asparagus spears
1 tbsp olive oil
juice of $\frac{1}{2}$ lemon
salt and freshly ground black pepper
2 tbsp chopped parsley (optional)

Cut the bok choy in half and remove any damaged leaves. Top and tail the beans. Trim off the hard ends of the asparagus, then cut each spear into three pieces.

Wash all the vegetables in cold water, then place them in a mixing bowl. Cover with boiling water, then drain after 5 minutes.

Heat the oil in a wok or non-stick pan. Stir-fry the vegetables for about 2 minutes. Add lemon juice, season with salt and pepper, add the parsley and serve.

Crisp Asian Vegetables with Oyster Sauce and Sesame Seeds

It's worthwhile getting to know the lovely flavours and textures of Chinese vegetables, which are often crunchy. It's fun to do a Chinese cookery course.

Serves 2

4 baby bok choy

1 small bunch Chinese broccoli

1 cup shredded Chinese cabbage

2 tbsp oyster sauce

$\frac{1}{2}$ tsp sesame oil

juice of $\frac{1}{2}$ lemon

freshly ground black pepper

1 tbsp sesame seeds

Halve the bok choy lengthwise. Trim off any damaged leaves, then wash the bok choy well in cold water.

Trim off the hard end part of the Chinese broccoli and any damaged leaves. Cut the broccoli into bite-size pieces, then wash in cold water.

Place all the vegetables in a saucepan of salted boiling water and boil for 2 or 3 minutes, then drain. Return the vegetables to the pan and add the oyster sauce, sesame oil and lemon juice. Season with a little pepper and toss well to coat the vegetables. Serve sprinkled with sesame seeds.

Green Asparagus with a Walnut and Olive Salsa

Select plump, firm, fresh-looking asparagus, remembering that it is a spring vegetable in temperate climates.

Serves 2

12 large green asparagus spears (more if they're thinner)
1 large tomato
1$\frac{1}{2}$ tbsp extra virgin olive oil
8 green or black olives, pitted and finely sliced
2 tbsp walnut halves, chopped
juice of $\frac{1}{2}$ medium-sized lemon
salt and freshly ground black pepper

Trim off the hard end of the asparagus spears. Peel about 5 cm (2 in) of the thickest part, then wash the spears in cold water.

Cut the tomato in half, squeeze out the seeds, then dice the flesh.

Cook the asparagus in a large amount of salted boiling water for 3 to 5 minutes until tender. Drain and place on plates.

As the asparagus cooks, heat the oil, tomato, olives and walnuts in a saucepan for 1 minute. Add the lemon juice and season with salt and pepper. Spoon the salsa over the asparagus and serve.

Silverbeet with Eggs

This delicious light meal consists of eggs and a good serving of silverbeet cooked like an omelette and served with bread or toast. The silverbeet can be cooked in advance.

Serves 2

1/2 bunch silverbeet (about 6 stalks)
1 tbsp olive oil
1/4 brown onion, chopped
1/2 clove garlic, chopped (optional)
salt and freshly ground black pepper
4 eggs, beaten

Trim off the thick, white stalks of the silverbeet. Wash and dry the silverbeet then shred it and place in a saucepan. Cover with a lid and cook the silverbeet in its own steam for 10 minutes. Drain and allow to cool slightly before squeezing out the excess moisture.

Heat the oil in a medium-sized frypan. Add the onion and cook for 2 minutes. Add the silverbeet and stir-fry for 2 minutes to heat it through. Stir in the garlic and season with salt and pepper.

Add the beaten eggs, stir briefly and allow the egg to cook. Serve hot with good bread.

Spicy Peas and Potatoes

Add other diced vegetables, such as pumpkin, carrots, tomatoes and capsicum, to this simple, tasty dish, and serve it with a green salad to make a light meal.

Serves 2

2 medium-sized potatoes, peeled and diced

1 tbsp vegetable oil

$\frac{1}{2}$ small onion, diced

$\frac{1}{4}$ tsp mustard seeds

$\frac{1}{4}$ tsp cumin seeds

$\frac{1}{2}$ tsp curry powder

$\frac{1}{4}$ tsp ground turmeric

salt and freshly ground black pepper

1 cup cooked peas

2 tbsp chopped parsley

Place the diced potato in a saucepan, cover with cold water and bring to the boil. Boil for 5 minutes, then drain.

Heat the oil in a wok or non-stick frypan. Stir in the onion, mustard seeds and cumin seeds and cook on a medium heat for about 2 minutes. Add the curry powder and turmeric. Stir in the potatoes, season with salt and pepper and stir-fry for 5 minutes. Add the peas and mix gently. Cook for 5 minutes or until the potatoes are soft.

Sprinkle with chopped parsley and serve.

Stir-fried Shiitake Mushrooms with Bok Choy

The texture of these two beautiful vegetables cooked together is fantastic, and the dish is most satisfying and refreshing.

Serves 2

6 small bok choy
8 fresh shiitake mushrooms
1 tbsp vegetable oil
$1/2$ clove garlic, finely chopped
1 tsp grated ginger
1 tsp cornflour mixed with 1 tbsp water
$1/2$ tbsp light soy sauce
a little chilli paste to taste

Wash the bok choy and slice finely. Wash and slice the mushrooms.

Heat the oil in a wok or non-stick frypan. Add the garlic and ginger and stir for 5 seconds before adding the mushrooms and bok choy. Stir-fry until the vegetables are tender.

Make a hole in the centre of the vegetables and pour the cornflour mixture and soy sauce into the pan. Stir well and toss with the vegetables. Add a little chilli paste and serve with rice or on its own.

Baked Celery and Carrots

This rustic vegetable dish appeals more to adults than to most young children. It makes a lovely, light dinner, especially when served with good bread.

Serves 4

1/2 bunch of celery

2 large carrots

2 tbsp olive oil

3 slices lean bacon, diced

1 brown onion, diced

1 clove garlic, crushed

2 cups strong chicken stock (see page 40) or beef stock

1/2 tbsp cornflour mixed with 2 tbsp white wine or water

freshly ground black pepper

4 tbsp chopped parsley

Preheat the oven to 180°C (350°F).

Trim off any damaged outer parts of the celery. Discard the leaves, then peel the outer stalks to remove large strings. Cut the celery into 5 cm (2 in) pieces.

Peel and dice the carrots.

Heat the oil in a flameproof casserole dish on the stove top. Add the bacon and onion and stir for 3–4 minutes. Add the carrot, celery, garlic and stock and bring to a simmer. Add the cornflour and wine mixture and stir for 1 minute. Season with pepper, cover with foil and a lid and bake in the preheated oven for 20–30 minutes or until the vegetables are tender.

Just before serving, stir in the parsley.

Eggplant Moussaka

This traditional, satisfying Greek dish takes about 2 hours to prepare and is a dish for confident cooks.

Serves 6

2 medium-sized to large eggplants

2 tbsp salt

4 tbsp olive oil

1 onion, finely chopped

2 cloves garlic, finely chopped

about 1 kg (2 lb) minced lamb or beef

1 tbsp tomato paste

1/2 cup dry white wine

400 g (14 oz) can diced tomatoes

1/4 tsp ground cinnamon

salt and freshly ground black pepper

60 g (2 oz) butter

50 g (1 1/2 oz) plain flour

2 cups milk

a little grated nutmeg

1 egg, lightly beaten

4 tbsp grated parmesan cheese

Freezing

It's really useful to have a supply of sauces, stocks and leftovers in the freezer.

Food should be wrapped tightly before freezing to prevent oxidisation. Freezer bags are great for this – it is easy to remove all the air and seal them tightly. Food in bags also freezes very quickly.

Frozen leftovers should be used within 4–6 weeks of being frozen.

Cut eggplants into 1.5 cm (½ in) round slices. Place in a bowl,
sprinkle with 2 tablespoons of salt and allow to stand for about
45 minutes.

Meanwhile, heat half the olive oil in a pan and stir-fry the onion
and garlic on a medium heat for about 5 minutes. Add the meat and
brown it on a high heat, stirring constantly. Add the tomato paste
and the wine and bring to a simmer. Add the diced tomato and the
cinnamon, season with salt and pepper and simmer for 35 minutes.

Briefly rinse the eggplant slices under the tap and dry with kitchen
paper.

Heat the remaining oil in a large, non-stick frypan and cook the
eggplant slices on each side for a few minutes, then drain.

Melt the butter in a small saucepan. Whisk in the flour and cook
on a low heat for 3 minutes. Increase the heat, add the milk little
by little and whisk until the sauce thickens. Lower the heat and
cook for 2 minutes more. Season with salt, pepper and nutmeg.

Preheat the oven to 150°C (300°F). Grease a 30 x 22 cm (12 x 8 in)
deep oven dish. Arrange half the eggplant slices in the bottom and
top with half the meat sauce. Add the remaining eggplant in a
layer and the remaining meat.

Whisk the egg and half the parmesan cheese into the white sauce
and spread over the meat. Sprinkle the top with the remaining
parmesan cheese and bake in the preheated oven for about 1 hour.

Remove from the oven and wait for 5–10 minutes before slicing.

Grilled Vegetables

Use either a large cast-iron or non-stick grill for the vegetables, or cook them in a large non-stick pan or on the barbecue. Adjust the quantities according to the number of people you are catering for.

A selection of vegetables, cut into regular 1 cm (½ in) slices.
  Vegetables to try include eggplant, zucchini, capsicum, fennel, butternut pumpkin, onion, mushrooms, sweet potatoes, tomatoes, artichokes, asparagus (cut in half).

a little olive oil

salt and freshly ground black pepper

a little oregano or lemon thyme, chopped

In a large bowl mix the olive oil (just sufficient to coat the vegetables lightly) with the oregano, salt and pepper. Toss the vegetables gently in this dressing.

Grill the vegetables on a medium heat for a few minutes on each side. Serve immediately or allow to cool, then store in the refrigerator for a salad or sandwich.

If you need to, you can reheat the vegetables in a hot oven at 200°C (400°F) for about 10 minutes.

Roast Mediterranean Vegetables

These vegetables are delicious either on their own, with good bread, served with polenta or tossed with pasta. They're also a lovely accompaniment to roast chicken, roast beef or a roast leg of lamb, but cook them in a separate oven dish if you want to prevent them from absorbing the saturated fat from the meat. Vary the vegetables according to your taste.

Serves 4

2 red capsicums

3 small eggplants

8 large button mushrooms

2 tbsp olive oil

1 tbsp lemon thyme, finely chopped

$\frac{1}{2}$ clove garlic, chopped, optional

salt and freshly ground black pepper

Preheat the oven to 220°C (425°F).

Halve, seed and wash the capsicums. Cut each half in two lengthwise and place in a large bowl. Wash the eggplants and trim off the stalks. Cut the eggplants into slices 3 cm (1 in) thick and add to the bowl. Wash the mushrooms and add to the bowl with the olive oil and lemon thyme.

Toss the vegetables well to coat them with oil then place them on a non-stick roasting tray. Roast in the preheated oven for 20–25 minutes, turning the vegetables during the cooking.

When the vegetables are cooked, stir in the garlic, season with salt and pepper and serve.

Red Cabbage and Apple

This delicious vegetable dish can be served either on its own or with roast or grilled pork or poultry.

Serves 4

about 1/3 red cabbage

1 tbsp peanut oil or polyunsaturated oil

2 apples (Granny Smith or Golden Delicious)

1 cup stock or water

salt and freshly ground black pepper

Trim off any damaged leaves and the stalk of the cabbage, then slice the cabbage finely.

Heat the oil on a medium heat in a non-stick saucepan or wok. Cook the sliced cabbage for about 5 minutes, stirring from time to time.

Meanwhile, peel, quarter, core and grate the apples. Mix the apple with the cabbage, then add the stock and season with salt and pepper. Bring to a simmer, cover and cook for about 30 minutes or until the cabbage is soft. Stir occasionally during the cooking.

Sautéed Field Mushrooms with Herbs

Choose large, fleshy, pale mushrooms. When field mushrooms are unavailable, use Swiss brown mushrooms or button mushrooms. Serve with a good wholemeal or sourdough bread, perhaps toasted.

Serves 2

about 300 g (10 oz) field mushrooms
1 tbsp olive oil
¼ brown onion, sliced
2 tsp chopped lemon thyme
salt and freshly ground black pepper
2 tbsp chopped parsley
½ clove garlic, finely chopped

Briefly wash the mushrooms in cold water, then cut them into 1.5 cm (½ in) slices.

Heat the oil in a large non-stick frypan. Place the mushrooms and onion in the hot pan, but don't move them for about 30 seconds. Toss the mushrooms and add the lemon thyme. Cook for 3–4 minutes, tossing occasionally.

Season with salt and pepper, parsley and garlic, toss well and serve.

Spinach and Ricotta Filo Tart

This easy, delicious tart is held together with filo pastry. The pastry base is very thin and it is moist when cold.

Serves 4–6

300 g (10 oz) fresh spinach

1 cup milk

2 tsp cornflour

2 eggs

250 g (8 oz) ricotta cheese

a pinch of chilli powder

a large pinch of grated nutmeg

1 tbsp grated parmesan cheese

salt and freshly ground black pepper

1 tbsp olive oil

3 sheets of filo pastry

Preheat the oven to 200°C (400°F).

Wash the spinach thoroughly and place it in a large saucepan. Cover the pan and cook the spinach on a medium heat for 3–5 minutes, stirring occasionally during the cooking. Drain the spinach and run cold water over it to cool it. Squeeze the spinach to remove as much water as possible, then chop it coarsely.

Combine the milk and cornflour in a small bowl.

In a large bowl whisk the eggs with the ricotta and the milk mixture until they are well combined. Stir in the chopped spinach with the chilli powder, nutmeg, parmesan, salt and pepper.

Brush a 22-cm (8-in) springform, loose-bottomed flan tin with a little oil, then line it with a sheet of filo pastry. Brush the pastry with a little oil and tuck the excess pastry round the edge of the tin. Place a second layer of pastry on top and brush with the remaining oil. Place the last layer of pastry on top, making sure the sides of the tin are covered with pastry.

Pour the cheese and spinach preparation into the tin, then carefully place the tin on a flat oven tray. Cook the tart in the preheated oven for about 25 minutes or until set.

Stuffed Eggplant

This Mediterranean dish is often prepared with minced pork or veal, but you can omit the meat if you prefer to keep it vegetarian. Choose evenly shaped eggplants.

Serves 2–4

2 medium-sized to large eggplants

3 tbsp olive oil

$\frac{1}{2}$ brown onion, chopped

1 tsp dried oregano

200 g (7 oz) minced meat (beef, veal, pork or chicken)

1 cup cooked rice

2 tbsp chopped parsley

1 clove garlic, finely chopped

a pinch of cayenne pepper

salt and freshly ground black pepper

3 tbsp fresh breadcrumbs

Preheat the oven to 200°C (400°F).

Wash the eggplants and cut them in half lengthwise. Make some criss-cross cuts about 1 cm deep into the flesh without cutting the skin. Brush the flesh with about one-third of the oil, then place the eggplants in a baking dish and bake for 20–25 minutes in the preheated oven until the flesh is soft enough to be scooped out.

Meanwhile, heat the remaining oil in a non-stick pan and stir-fry the onion on a medium heat for 5 minutes. Increase the heat, add the oregano and mince and stir-fry until the mince changes colour. Stir in the rice, parsley, garlic and cayenne pepper and season with salt and pepper. Turn off the heat.

Carefully scoop out the eggplant flesh and mix it into the mince preparation. Spoon the mixture back into the eggplant shells and sprinkle the top with breadcrumbs. Bake in the oven for about 20 minutes then serve.

Zucchini Gratin

Serves 2

6 small zucchini, about 12 cm (5 in) long
$\frac{1}{2}$ tbsp olive oil
1 tsp finely chopped thyme
freshly ground black pepper
2 tbsp breadcrumbs
1 tbsp parmesan cheese
$\frac{1}{2}$ clove garlic, finely chopped
$\frac{1}{2}$ cup Italian-style tomato sauce, bottled or home-made
(see page 84)

Wash the zucchini and trim away the stalk ends. Cook them in
salted boiling water for 2 minutes, then drain. Halve the zucchini
lengthwise.

Heat the oil in a non-stick frypan. Add the zucchini and thyme
and cook on moderate heat for a few minutes on each side until
soft. Transfer the zucchini to a gratin dish and season with salt
and pepper.

Heat the grill.

Mix the breadcrumbs with the parmesan cheese and garlic.

Spoon the tomato sauce over the zucchini and sprinkle with the
breadcrumb preparation. Cook under a hot grill until hot and
lightly browned.

Jerusalem Artichoke Purée

Choose large unblemished and unwrinkled Jerusalem artichokes for this delicate purée. Serve with roast or grilled fish or meat.

Serves 4

600–800 g (1$\frac{1}{4}$–1$\frac{1}{2}$ lb) Jerusalem artichokes
juice of $\frac{1}{2}$ lemon
1 cup chicken or vegetable stock (see pages 40 and 41), or water
a pinch of salt
freshly ground black pepper
1 tbsp olive oil
2 tbsp chopped parsley or snipped chives

Cut the Jerusalem artichokes into 3 cm (1 in) pieces and peel each piece, placing it immediately into cold water mixed with lemon juice. This stops the vegetable from turning brown.

Place the artichoke pieces in a saucepan with the stock and season with salt and pepper. Cover with foil inside the pan and a lid and cook until the artichokes are soft, stirring occasionally during the cooking.

Blend to a purée, adding a little cooking liquid if it is too thick.

Stir in the olive oil and parsley just before serving.

POTATOES

Buying and Storing

Ask your greengrocer for the variety that is best suited to your
plans. Some fruit shops and supermarkets may even have some
printed information available.

Choose firm, unblemished potatoes, and avoid potatoes that are
wet, have green spots on the skin or are sprouting. Make sure that
they are regular in shape and size, for example, use long potatoes for
wedges, small ones for salads.

New potatoes, i.e. those that are harvested early in a crop, have a
thin skin and are not necessarily small in size. They are lovely boiled
or steamed, and need to be eaten within a few days. Potatoes with dirt
left on them will keep longer (a couple of weeks).

Store potatoes in a dark, well-ventilated spot, such as a cupboard
or cellar. Don't refrigerate raw potatoes and avoid keeping them in a
warm room. Store in a basket or in a fabric or paper bag, but avoid
plastic.

Potato varieties and their uses

Bintje, Coliban, Desirée, Gold Star, Nicola, Pontiac, Sebago, Spunta, Symfonia	**Mashing**
Desirée, Kipfler, Nicola, Pink Fir Apple, Pontiac, Sebago, Spunta	**Salad or boiling**
Bintje, Coliban, Desirée, Gold Star, Idaho, Latona, Royal Blue, Sebago, Spunta	**Roasting**
Kipfler, Pink Fir Apple, Bintje, Desirée, Coliban, Sebago	**Microwaving**
Sebago, Royal Blue, Purple Congo, Idaho	**Frying**
Bintje, Royal Blue, Sebago, Symfonia, Idaho, Gold Star, Desirée Coliban	**Baking**

Boiled Potatoes

IS IT COOKED?

Experience is very important in understanding when food is cooked. Cookbooks and recipes can only give an idea – you need to learn to recognise the signs that help you know that the food is cooked. It's important to pay attention to small details, like the change of colour or texture that occurs when food cooks – the change in texture of potatoes is a great example of this. Use a recipe as a guide, but take charge of the dish, and before serving, double-check that the food is cooked appropriately.

For 2 people, brush 6–8 small potatoes under cold running water. Place the cleaned potatoes in saucepan, 4 cups cold water and add a pinch of salt. Place on a high to medium heat, bring to the boil and cook for about 15 minutes or until you can easily pierce them with the tip of a blade.

Drain the potatoes in a colander, then place them on serving plates. If you are not eating them hot, cool them in cold water, drain and refrigerate.

Mashed Potato

To obtain a smooth texture, I prefer to use a hand-operated mouli. Alternatively, use a hand masher. You can use olive oil instead of butter to avoid saturated fats, and soy milk instead of milk if you have problems with dairy products.

Serves 4

about 600 g (1 1/4 lb) medium-sized potatoes
2/3 cup milk
30 g (1 oz) butter, cut into small pieces
salt and freshly ground black pepper

Peel and quarter the potatoes. Place in a pan, cover with cold water and season with salt. Bring to the boil and cook until just done. Drain in a colander.

Heat the milk in a saucepan large enough to hold the mashed potato.

Pass the drained potatoes through a mouli into the saucepan holding the hot milk. Using a wooden spoon, mix the potato and milk until smooth. Add the butter and mix well. Season with salt and pepper and serve.

Italian-style Baked Potatoes

Easy to prepare and full of Mediterranean flavour. Use large
potatoes, such as Bintje, Desirée or Spunta varieties.

Serves 4

1½ tbsp olive oil

4 large potatoes

2 cloves garlic, crushed

1 tbsp fresh rosemary leaves

1 tsp sea salt

freshly ground black pepper

Preheat the oven to 220°C (425°F).

Cover the base of a metal baking dish, preferably non-stick, with
olive oil and place it in the oven for 2–3 minutes.

Peel the potatoes and cut them into 2.5 cm (1 in) cubes. Place the
potatoes in the hot oil and sprinkle with the crushed garlic and
rosemary. Bake the potatoes for 40 minutes, tossing two or three
times. Reduce the heat if necessary.

In the final 10 minutes of the cooking, sprinkle the potatoes with
sea salt and season with a little pepper.

Indian-style Potato and Pumpkin Casserole with Chickpeas

Once you understand the principle of this dish, you'll be able to create others using different vegetables and spices.

Serves 4–6

$1/2$ onion, peeled

3 cm (1 in) piece of ginger, peeled

2 cloves garlic, peeled

$1/2$ tbsp peanut oil

about 8 fennel seeds

$1/2$ tsp black mustard seeds

$1/3$ of a star anise

2 cardamom pods

1 tsp coriander seeds

$1/3$ of a small red chilli

1 cm ($1/2$ in) piece cinnamon stick

1 tsp ground turmeric

1 tsp ground cumin

1 tsp ground coriander

2 medium-sized potatoes, cubed

4 tomatoes, cut into small pieces

100 g ($3^1/2$ oz) button mushrooms, halved

$1/2$ red capsicum, cut into small pieces

2 cups butternut pumpkin, cubed

salt and freshly ground black pepper

400 g (14 oz) can chickpeas

Blend the onion, ginger and garlic to a paste in a small processor.

Heat the oil in a non-stick saucepan, stir in the onion paste and fry on a medium heat for 2 minutes. Add the fennel and mustard seeds, star anise, cardamom pods, coriander seeds, chilli and cinnamon and stir for 2 minutes. Add the ground turmeric, cumin and coriander and stir well. Add the potato and stir for 2 minutes before adding the tomato, mushroom, capsicum and pumpkin. Season with salt and pepper, stir well, cover with a lid and cook on a low heat for 20 minutes, stirring occasionally.

Add the drained chickpeas and cook for a further 5 minutes.

Dried or Canned Beans and Chickpeas?

For any of the recipes in this book you can replace canned beans with dried beans that you have soaked and cooked yourself. Soak dried beans in plenty of cold water for up to 24 hours then cook them in boiling water until tender. The cooking time will vary, depending on the type and age of the bean.

Bean and Potato Curry

Serves 4

300 g (10 oz) green beans
4 medium-sized potatoes
2 tbsp vegetable oil
$\frac{1}{2}$ brown onion, finely chopped
2 tsp finely grated ginger
2 cloves garlic, finely chopped
$\frac{1}{2}$ tsp mustard seeds
1 tsp coriander seeds
1 cardamom pod
$\frac{1}{2}$ tbsp medium-strength curry powder
$\frac{1}{2}$ cup Italian-style tomato sauce, bottled or home-made
(see page 84)
1 cup boiling water or hot chicken stock (see page 40)
150 g (5 oz) button mushrooms
salt and freshly ground black pepper
$\frac{1}{2}$ cup coconut cream or extra Italian-style tomato sauce
$\frac{1}{2}$ cup chopped coriander leaves
$\frac{1}{2}$ tsp chilli paste (optional)

Top and tail the beans, then cut them into bite-sized pieces.
Peel the potatoes and cut them into 2 cm (1 in) cubes.

Bring a large pot of water to the boil. Add the beans and boil for
about 3 minutes. Add the potato, boil for 2 minutes, then drain.

Heat the oil in a wok or large non-stick pan. Stir-fry the onion,
ginger and garlic on medium heat for 2 minutes. Add the
mustard seeds, coriander seeds and cardamom and stir-fry for
1 minute. Stir in the curry powder and add the tomato sauce,
water, potato, beans and mushrooms, and season with salt and
pepper. Stir well and cook, covered with a lid, for about
5 minutes, stirring two or three times during the cooking.

Stir in the coconut cream and continue to cook, uncovered, until
the potato is cooked.

Just before serving, stir in the chopped coriander leaves and chilli
paste. Serve with rice.

Baked Sliced Potatoes the Hungarian Way

A delicious, low-fat potato dish.

Serves 4

600 g (1¼ lb) potatoes
1 tbsp olive oil
1 small brown onion, chopped
1 tbsp finely chopped thyme
2 tomatoes, chopped
2 tsp ground sweet paprika
2 cups chicken stock (see page 40), broth or water
freshly ground black pepper
a pinch of salt
3 tbsp chopped parsley

Peel the potatoes and cut them into 5 mm (¼ in) slices.

Preheat the oven to 180°C (350°F).

Heat the oil in a small pan and fry the onion and thyme until the onion has softened. Add the tomatoes, paprika, stock and a little pepper and salt and bring to the boil.

Arrange the potato slices in an oiled oven dish and cover with the tomato preparation. Bake in the preheated oven for about 30 minutes or until the potato is cooked. Sprinkle with chopped parsley before serving.

Potato Gnocchi

You can flavour
this basic gnocchi
recipe with
chopped herbs
such as parsley
or basil, or with
chopped cooked
spinach.

Gnocchi are fun and relatively simple to make. The secret for
light gnocchi is to obtain the right balance between the mashed
potato and the flour – too much flour and the gnocchi are heavy;
not enough flour and they don't hold together well. You'll master
it after a few tries.

Serves 4

2 large potatoes, about 500–600 g (1–1¼ lb) in total
about 1½ cups plain flour
a little salt

Wash the potatoes. Place the whole potatoes in a saucepan, cover
with cold water and add a little salt. Bring to the boil and cook
for 25–40 minutes, depending on their size.

Peel the potatoes and mash using a mouli over a bowl.

Using your fingers, slowly incorporate the flour bit by bit into the
mashed potato until you have a smooth paste, not too soft, not
too dry and perhaps a little sticky. Depending on the moisture
content of the potatoes, you may not need to use all the flour.

Lightly flour your work bench and knead the potato paste with
the heel of your hand, as when making bread or pastry. Don't be
hesitant about it. Fold the dough over onto itself and push it
away from you. This makes the dough elastic. Some cooks like to
knead with both hands and 5 minutes of kneading should do the
job.

Cut dough into four or five pieces and cover them with a tea
towel.

Roll one piece of dough into a snake shape about 2 cm (¾ in)
thick, then cut this into 2 cm (¾ in) lengths. Dust one hand with
flour and dip a table fork into flour as well.

Now take one of the gnocchi (a gnoccho) and press your well-
floured index finger gently into it. Roll the gnoccho along the
inside prongs of the fork to make a pattern of lines on it. Your
first ones may not be perfect but after a few you'll get the knack
of it. Once you have made all your gnocchi, keep them covered
with a cloth or plastic film. Their special shape allows the
gnocchi to cook evenly and helps the sauce coat them well.

Cook the gnocchi in a large amount of salted boiling water. They cook very quickly (in just a few minutes) and are ready as soon as they float to the surface. Remove them with a slotted spoon.

Serve with an Italian-style tomato sauce (see page 84), pesto (see page 194) or spicy veal sauce (see page 246).

The Timing of an Everyday Meal

Before cooking a meal, rehearse in your mind the major steps – 'I must boil the potatoes, steam the beans and pan-fry the fish fillet.'

Establish which part of the meal will take the longest to prepare and start with that. Then continue with the second longest part.

Sometimes you can start by cooking something that can be prepared in advance and reheated at the last minute, such as a soup, rice dish or stew.

It's best to cook pan-fried or grilled fish, meat or burgers just before serving.

You can keep many cooked foods warm for a short time covered in foil in a low oven (100°C, 200°F).

Cooked vegetables can be kept warm in a steamer with the heat turned off and the lid on the pan.

It's easy to reheat most foods, including rice, vegetables, pasta, potatoes, stews, soups and stir-fries, in the microwave for a short time (see your microwave instructions).

For stir-fry dishes, soups, stews and curries, do most of the cutting and chopping of vegetables and condiments before you start cooking.

Be realistic about the time it takes to prepare a simple, complete meal from beginning to end. For example, for mashed potatoes, boiled peas and pan-fried chicken fillets, it takes between 30 and 45 minutes whether you are experienced and fast or not, even when someone helps you.

Meatless Tacos

Something flavoursome to satisfy those who prefer not to eat meat. You can prepare most of this dish a day or two ahead.

Makes 6 tacos

1 small to medium-sized carrot, peeled and finely diced

1/2 cup diced pumpkin

1 tbsp olive oil

1/2 brown onion, finely chopped

1/2 green chilli, seeded and chopped

1 small clove garlic, finely chopped

1 tsp ground sweet paprika

1/2 tsp ground coriander

1 tsp ground cumin

1 tbsp tomato paste

400 g (14 oz) can lentils, drained

1/2 cup water

1/2 tsp salt

freshly ground black pepper

2 tbsp chopped coriander leaves

6 taco shells

1 cup shredded lettuce

2 tomatoes, diced

1/2 cup grated Swiss cheese

Steam or microwave the carrot and pumpkin until soft.

Heat the oil in a wok or non-stick pan and stir-fry the onion for 2 minutes. Add the chilli and garlic and stir well. Add the paprika, coriander, cumin, tomato paste, carrot, pumpkin and drained lentils.

Cover with water, bring to a simmer and cook gently for 10 minutes. Then season with salt and pepper and stir in the chopped coriander leaves.

Heat the taco shells in the oven at 150°C (300°F) for about 5 minutes.

Everyone can garnish their own tacos or you can spoon some lentil preparation into the shells, then top with some lettuce, diced tomato and grated cheese. Serve immediately or the shells will become soggy.

Mixed Curried Vegetables

Make this dish in a wok or non-stick saucepan and use your
favourite vegetables – there are very few that don't work in
a curry. Serve with rice.

Serves 4

2 tbsp oil, e.g. peanut, sunflower

1/2 onion, chopped

1 clove garlic, chopped

1/2 tsp mustard seeds

1/2 tsp caraway seeds

2 tsp curry powder

1 tsp turmeric

3 tomatoes, chopped

1 cup cauliflower florets

1 cup shelled peas

2 zucchini, cut into 3 cm (1 in) pieces

400 g (14 oz) can chickpeas, drained

salt and freshly ground black pepper

1 cup coriander leaves

Heat the oil in a wok.

Add the onion, garlic, mustard seeds and caraway seeds and stir
on a low heat for 2 minutes. Stir in the curry powder and
turmeric. Add the tomatoes and stir well. Add the cauliflower,
peas, zucchini and chickpeas and season with salt and pepper.

Stir well, cover with a lid and cook, stirring occasionally, for
10–15 minutes until the vegetables are soft.

Sprinkle with coriander leaves and serve.

Hints with Herbs

Add herbs at the end of the cooking. Except for rosemary, thyme, bayleaves and sometimes parsley, most herbs are best added to a dish just before serving, as 'fines herbes', such as basil, coriander, chives, etc. lose much of their flavour when boiled or exposed to strong heat.

Preparing herbs. Remove any damaged leaves and trim off any hard or dried stalks. Wash the herbs briefly in a bowl of cold water or under the tap. Dry them gently using a clean cloth, absorbent paper or a salad dryer.

Storing herbs. Fresh herbs such as parsley, basil, coriander, chives, tarragon, thyme and rosemary keep well for at least 5 days in the refrigerator. Store herbs loose either in a plastic bag or box, or in a glass jar with a lid.

Basil is a warmly flavoured, aromatic herb with wide, delicate leaves. It is wonderful with Mediterranean-style foods, especially pasta. Basil is used in a traditional pesto. Only the leaves are used, either whole in a salad or finely sliced and sprinkled over grilled fish, chopped in a pesto or to season food.

Bay leaf has a strong, sharp flavour and is used to infuse liquids and stews. Use the same quantity of fresh or dried leaves – half a bay leaf or one small bayleaf is sufficient to flavour a stew or stock for six to eight people. The bay leaf is usually removed before serving as its texture is unpleasant.

Bouquet garni is a French expression meaning a small bunch of herbs, usually made up of a few sprigs of parsley, one or two sprigs of thyme and a bay leaf, tied together with kitchen string. A bouquet garni is used in casseroles, stews, stocks and sauces, and is added at the start of the cooking.

Chives are a long, green herb that is usually cut into small pieces, using scissors or a knife. It is a great salad herb and is also used sprinkled over vegetables, fish, chicken or egg dishes. The flavour vanishes when it is exposed to excessive heat.

Coriander has leaves that closely resemble those of flat parsley, but are more fragile. Coriander is delicious in Asian dishes from salads to stir-fries and casseroles and it has a powerful, aromatic, slightly bitter flavour.

Dill is a fragile, anise-flavoured, dark-green herb that looks like fennel and is excellent with fish dishes, especially salmon and trout. It's also a nice accompaniment to vegetables, such as tomatoes, cucumber and asparagus. Rather than being chopped, delicate dill is usually snipped into small pieces, using scissors or a knife.

Mint is added to salads, fish and some meat dishes for its refreshing flavour. The leaves can be used whole or finely cut, rather than chopped.

Parsley adds a fresh flavour when sprinkled on most types of food, from salads to casseroles, and it helps to reduce the use of added salt. Flat parsley is more flavoursome than the curly variety and is the one used in the Middle Eastern tabouli salad.

Sage is a favourite herb for use in stuffings or for seasoning roast pork or veal. The flavour is robust, so just a few leaves are sufficient to season a dish for four people.

Tarragon is one of my favourite seasonings for chicken, with its long, narrow, delicate leaves and warm, slightly anise flavour. Once detached from the stalk, the leaves can be used whole or cut (not chopped) into small pieces. Tarragon is lovely mixed with other 'fines herbes', such as chives, parsley and basil, or to flavour a salad, omelette or vegetables.

Thyme is an easy-to-grow herb with several varieties; some have a lemony flavour, some are more peppery. Thyme is used in cooking, rather than being sprinkled on food. A sprig can be added to a casserole, it can be chopped and added to a marinade or added at the beginning of the cooking when pan-frying fish, chicken, chops, steak, etc.

Rosemary is a strongly flavoured herb that is perfect when marinating large joints of meat, such as roast lamb and beef, and is added at the beginning of the cooking, rather than at the end. It grows well in temperate regions.

Grilled Basil and Olive Polenta

Once you've mastered making polenta (and it is easy), you'll be able to adapt the seasoning (herbs, spices, etc.) to your taste.

Serves 4

1 cup polenta
salt and freshly ground black pepper
2 tbsp chopped parsley
2 tbsp chopped basil
2 tbsp freshly grated parmesan cheese
2 tbsp pitted black olives, cut into small pieces
about 2 tbsp olive oil

Cook the polenta according to the packet instructions. Season with salt and pepper and stir in the parsley, basil, grated parmesan and olives.

Spread the polenta on a shallow tray (about 20 x 30 cm, 8 x 12 in) lined with baking paper. Allow the polenta to set then cut into twelve rectangles and brush with a little olive oil.

Cook the polenta on a grill plate or barbecue and serve immediately. It is good served with a salad of mixed bitter leaves.

SAUCES

A sauce is to savoury food what icing is to cake – it provides a special touch indeed! The sauces on the following pages are good for many purposes: serve them over steamed vegetables or with fish or chicken for a simple meal.

Lemon Tahini Salsa

This flavoursome dressing is a good source of calcium because of the sesame which the tahini is made from. I love the slightly bitter taste. Serve over grilled fish, chicken or vegetables.

Serves 1

1 small tomato

1 tsp tahini (sesame seed paste)

2 tsp lemon juice (about $1/4$ lemon)

1 tbsp cold water

$1/4$ clove of garlic, chopped (optional)

1 tbsp chopped parsley, coriander or basil

salt and freshly ground black pepper

Remove the core of the tomato. Halve the tomato, scoop out the seeds, then dice it.

Whisk the tahini, lemon juice and water in a bowl. Stir in the tomato, garlic and herbs. Season to taste with salt and pepper and serve.

Cold Spicy Mexican Salsa

Make this sauce whenever you have a supply of tasty tomatoes.
Serve it with grilled or barbecued fish, vegetables or chicken.

Serves 4

3 large tomatoes
1 long green chilli
¼ tsp sea salt
freshly ground black pepper
juice of 1 medium-sized lime
½ tbsp olive oil
1 small red onion, finely diced
1 clove garlic, finely chopped
½ cup coriander leaves

Wash the tomatoes and remove the cores. Halve them and gently
squeeze out the seeds before dicing the tomatoes finely.

Remove the chilli stem, then halve the chilli and remove the
seeds. Slice the chilli finely and place in a bowl with the salt, a
little pepper and the lime juice. Stir briefly and add the tomatoes,
oil, onion, garlic and coriander. Stir again and serve.

If you are not going to use the salsa within 30 minutes, cover and
refrigerate it, but it is best not to prepare it too long before
serving as the dressing will lose its freshness.

Peanut Sauce

In Indonesia, peanut sauce is served with many vegetable dishes and salads and with satays of all kinds (see page 253).

Serves 4

2 cm piece ginger

$^1/_2$ small onion

1 clove garlic

3 cm piece tender lemongrass

1 tbsp peanut oil

$^1/_2$ tsp curry powder

2 tsp fish sauce or soy sauce

2 tbsp crunchy peanut butter

$^1/_2$ tsp chilli paste

$^3/_4$ cup coconut milk

In a food processor or blender, blend the ginger, onion and garlic to a purée or, if you prefer, chop them finely. Slice the lemongrass very finely.

In a small, non-stick saucepan gently fry the onion mixture in the oil on a low heat for 5 minutes, stirring with a wooden spoon to prevent burning. Add the lemongrass and stir for 2 minutes. Add the curry powder and fish sauce or soy sauce, and stir well before adding the peanut butter and chilli paste. Stir again.

Add the coconut milk to the sauce and stir well until smooth. Cook on a low heat for 2 minutes. It's now ready to serve.

Note: If the sauce is too thick, add a little hot water. If it's too thin, add some extra peanut butter.

White Sauce

You can remove lumps from your white sauce by beating it with a whisk or pushing it through a strainer.

Although seen as slightly old-fashioned, a basic white sauce is a good one to learn. Serve it over cauliflower with cheese, or use it in lasagna, moussaka and other favourite dishes.

Serves 4–6

60 g (2 oz) butter

50 g (1½ oz) plain flour

2 cups milk

a little grated nutmeg

salt and freshly ground black pepper

a pinch of cayenne pepper

Melt the butter in a small saucepan on a medium heat. Whisk in the flour and cook for 2 minutes, stirring constantly to avoid burning. Add the milk bit by bit and stir well. Bring to the boil and allow to simmer slowly for 10 minutes. Stir occasionally to prevent sticking. Season with nutmeg, salt, pepper and cayenne.

Curry Sauce for a Vegetable Dish

This is a handy sauce to learn to make for serving with leftover vegetables (such as beans, broccoli and cauliflower) or to add to lentils or other beans to create a delicious vegetarian dish.

Serves 4

1 tbsp vegetable oil

$1/2$ tsp mustard seeds

$1/2$ tsp aniseed or fennel seeds

$1/2$ brown onion, chopped

1 clove garlic, chopped

1 tbsp grated ginger

1 tbsp curry powder

400 g (14 oz) can chopped tomatoes

salt and freshly ground black pepper

1 tsp ground cumin

2 tbsp chopped coriander leaves

Heat the oil on a medium heat in a non-stick saucepan or wok. Stir in the mustard seeds and aniseed or fennel seeds, then add the onion, garlic and ginger and cook without browning for 5 minutes.

Stir in the curry powder and cook for 30 seconds before adding the tomatoes. Stir well and simmer for 10 minutes.

Season with salt and pepper and stir in the cumin and coriander just before serving.

Serve with enough cooked vegetables for 4 people.

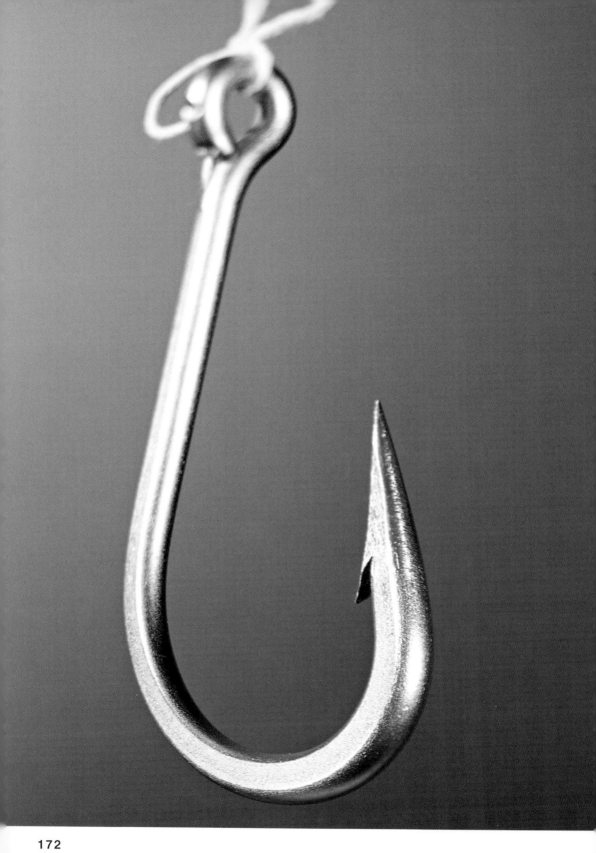

FISH

Fish is an exquisite food. I love it for its delicate texture and sublime flavour. Health experts want us to consume it regularly and they praise it for its protein, low-fat content and its ability to reduce the risk of heart disease and other illnesses.

At home, the best way to cook a fish fillet is often simply by pan-frying it in a minimum of oil in a non-stick pan, or by cooking it under the grill, then serving it with a squeeze of lemon. If you wish, the fillets can be coated lightly with plain flour, which gives them an appetising golden colour. But fish can be done in many other ways, as you will discover in this chapter. In the interests of good health, avoid eating or cooking deep-fried fish regularly – keep it as a treat a few times a year. See the information about how to recognise a good fishmonger and how to shop for fish and seafood on pages 16–17.

Grilled Crumbed Fish

Use long, flat fillets, such as whiting, sole or snapper. The breadcrumbs need to be very fine. Serve with a mixed salad of greens and steamed potatoes.

Serves 2

2 slices bread

4 sprigs of parsley

1 small clove garlic

$\frac{1}{4}$ tsp ground sweet paprika

salt and freshly ground black pepper

a pinch of cayenne pepper (optional)

2 white fish fillets

1 tbsp olive oil, melted butter or margarine

2 lemon wedges

Place the bread in a food processor with the parsley, garlic, paprika, salt, pepper and cayenne pepper and blend until the bread is in fine crumbs. Transfer to a plate.

Pat the fish dry, then brush with the oil or butter.

Coat the fish well on both sides with breadcrumbs. Place the fillets on an oiled baking sheet and cook under a preheated grill for several minutes on each side. Serve with lemon wedges.

Middle Eastern-style Fish Burgers

Middle Eastern seasonings of cumin, chilli and fresh coriander go well with chopped or minced fish in a burger, but the fish must be very fresh and the burger cooked at the last moment.

Serves 2

250 g (8 oz) boneless, skinless fish fillets

1 tbsp mayonnaise

2 tbsp chopped parsley or coriander leaves

1 tbsp finely chopped shallots

$1/4$ tsp ground cumin

$1/4$ tsp chilli sauce

salt and freshly ground black pepper

1 tbsp olive oil

2 bread rolls

2 tbsp tahini (sesame seed paste)

$1/2$ cup shredded lettuce

1 tomato, cut into 6 slices

Slice the fish thinly. Cut the slices into thin strips, then into small squares. Place in a mixing bowl with the mayonnaise, herbs, shallots, cumin and chilli sauce, and season with a little salt and pepper. Combine well, then refrigerate for 30 minutes.

Form the fish into two burgers.

Heat the oil in a pan and carefully cook the burgers for 4–5 minutes on each side.

Halve the bread rolls and toast them. Spread tahini on each half. Top two halves with shredded lettuce, the fish burgers and tomato. Replace the other half of each roll and eat immediately.

Grilled Fish with Salsa Verde

SALSA VERDE VARIATIONS

Create your own version of salsa verde, using vinegar instead of lemon and a different type of oil, for example, peanut, walnut or sunflower oil. You can use any of your favourite herbs and you can replace the capers with chopped gherkin or chopped anchovy fillets if you prefer. Salsa Verde is also delicious with finely sliced cold roast beef or pork, and vegetables such as aparagus and artichokes.

Salsa verde (green sauce) is a flavoursome dressing for grilled fish and meat. The capers can be replaced by gherkins or one or two chopped anchovy fillets.

Serves 2

2 fillets, each about 150 g (5 oz) of John Dory, snapper, flathead, barramundi or salmon

2 tbsp olive oil

freshly ground black pepper

juice of a small lemon

$1/2$ tsp prepared mustard of your choice

about 3 tbsp chopped parsley

2 mint leaves, chopped

1 tbsp chopped dill

$1/2$ tbsp capers

salt

Coat the fish fillets with half a tablespoon of the olive oil and season with black pepper.

In a bowl, mix the lemon juice with the mustard. Slowly whisk in the remaining oil. Add chopped parsley, mint and dill and the capers. Season with salt and pepper.

Cook the fillets on a hot grill or in a non-stick pan for about $2^1/2$ minutes on each side. Spoon the green dressing onto plates, top with the grilled fish and serve.

Pan-fried Salmon with Spinach and Bean Shoots

Atlantic salmon is an occasional family treat at our place. Its 'meaty' texture means that a small serve is enough, so it is reasonably affordable.

Serves 2

150 g (5 oz) bean shoots

juice of $\frac{1}{2}$ lemon

$\frac{1}{2}$ tsp soy sauce

3 drops sesame oil

300 g (10 oz) baby spinach

2 tbsp olive oil

2 pieces of salmon fillet, each 120–150 g (4–5 oz)

salt and freshly ground black pepper

$\frac{1}{2}$ clove garlic, finely chopped

Remove any damaged bean shoots.

Combine the lemon juice, soy sauce and sesame oil in a bowl.

Wash the spinach, then cook it for a few minutes in a large covered pan until wilted. Transfer the spinach to a colander and squeeze out the excess moisture.

Heat half the olive oil in a small, non-stick frypan and cook the salmon for about 2 minutes on each side. Season the fish with salt and pepper and cover with foil to keep it warm.

Heat the remaining olive oil in a large, non-stick frypan or wok. Stir in the garlic, then add the bean shoots and spinach and stir-fry for a few minutes. Season with pepper. Transfer the vegetables to a plate and top with the fish.

Spoon the lemon, soy and sesame dressing over the fish and spinach and serve immediately.

Take care not to overcook the salmon, as it dries quickly. The secret lies in cooking it, then allowing it to rest, during which time the heat goes to the centre without drying it out. You can also use another fish, such as ocean trout, tuna or blue eye.

Fresh Sardines au Gratin

This Provençal dish is very simple to make. Ask your fishmonger to gut and scale the sardines and to remove the heads. You can also use pilchards or other small fish, or fillets of flathead or whiting. Serve with a mixed salad.

Serves 2

8–12 medium-sized cleaned sardines
1$\frac{1}{2}$ tbsp olive oil
salt and freshly ground black pepper
$\frac{1}{2}$ cup fresh breadcrumbs
2 tbsp finely chopped parsley
$\frac{1}{2}$ clove garlic, very finely chopped
2 lemon quarters

Preheat the oven grill.

Place the cleaned sardines in a suitable gratin dish (porcelain, glass or metal). Drizzle the olive oil over the fish and season with a little salt and pepper. Sprinkle the breadcrumbs evenly over the sardines.

Place the sardines under the preheated grill and cook for 5–10 minutes or until they are ready, keeping an eye on them so that the breadcrumbs don't burn.

Mix together the parsley and garlic, sprinkle on the fish and serve with lemon wedges.

Carefully separate the flesh from the bones as you eat.

Fragrant Thai Fish Cakes

It is easier to prepare these fish cakes using a food processor.
If you don't have one, chop the fish on a chopping board, using
a large knife.

Serves 4 (makes 8–12 fish cakes)

about 600 g (1¼ lb) firm white fish fillets, e.g. flathead, gurnard,
  John Dory
¾ cup coriander leaves
2 tsp cornflour
1 large egg, beaten
2 tbsp fish sauce
2 tbsp very cold water
2 tsp red curry paste
2 dried or fresh kaffir lime leaves, very finely sliced then chopped
3 spring onions, very finely sliced
about 2 cups vegetable oil for deep frying
1 lime, quartered, or some Asian Sweet Chilli Dipping Sauce
  (opposite)

Place the fish in the food processor with the coriander leaves and
blend in short bursts of about 2 seconds until the fish is just
mushy. Don't over-process or the fish will become warm and lose
its freshness.

Add the cornflour, egg, fish sauce, cold water and curry paste and
blend until they are just combined. Transfer the mixture to a
bowl and stir in the lime leaves and spring onion. Refrigerate for
15 minutes.

Using cold, wet hands, form about 2 tablespoons of the mixture
into a small ball, then flatten it into a patty. Do the same with the
remaining mixture.

Heat the oil in a frypan and deep-fry the fish cakes for about
3 minutes until they are well browned and cooked. Drain on
kitchen paper and serve with lime quarters or a dipping sauce.

Asian Sweet Chilli Dipping Sauce

This light but flavoursome sauce is delicious with fish cakes or green vegetables such as asparagus or bok choy.

Serves about 4

1/3 cup water

2 tbsp caster sugar

1 tbsp white wine vinegar

2 tbsp fish sauce

1 clove garlic, finely chopped

1/2 cup finely diced cucumber, peeled and seeds removed

1 tbsp sweet chilli sauce

1 tsp finely chopped mint

1 tbsp finely chopped coriander leaves

Boil the water and sugar for 3 minutes. Allow to cool completely.

Stir in the vinegar, fish sauce, garlic, cucumber, chilli sauce, mint and coriander. Serve or cover with plastic wrap and refrigerate.

Spicy Flathead Stew

Flathead is a firm, tasty and affordable fish which makes a good choice for this hearty, Mediterranean-style dish. You could also use gurnard or leatherjacket. Ask your fishmonger to clean and scale the fish, to remove the head and cut the fish into 5 cm (2 in) sections. These will still contain bones, so if you are making the dish for children, ask your fishmonger for fillets instead.

Serves 4

1 medium-sized bulb of fennel

2 sticks celery

2 tbsp olive oil

1 small green chilli, halved, seeds removed then finely sliced

1/2 brown onion, chopped

400 g (14 oz) can diced tomatoes

a pinch of saffron or 1/4 tsp ground turmeric

1 bay leaf, dried or fresh

salt and freshly ground black pepper

1.5 kg (3 lb) flathead or gurnard

boiling water from the kettle

2 cloves garlic, finely chopped

Trim the fennel stalk, then dice the fennel. Dice the celery.

Heat the oil in a wok or large non-stick saucepan. Add the chilli, onion, fennel and celery and stir-fry for a few minutes. Add the tomato and bring to the boil. Stir in the saffron and bay leaf and season with salt and pepper.

Add the fish pieces and shake the pan briefly. Add a little boiling water to just cover the fish. Bring to the boil and cook quickly without stirring for about 12 minutes.

Gently stir in the garlic and serve with good bread. Eat with care as there will be bones in the fish.

Spicy Stir-fried Fish
with Chinese Broccoli

Refreshing and quick to prepare, this dish can be adapted by using whichever fish and Asian greens you prefer. Ask your fishmonger to remove the skin and bones of the fish.

Serves 2

about 2 cups Chinese broccoli, thinly cut into bite-sized pieces
1 tbsp vegetable oil
2 spring onions, cut into 2 cm (1 in) pieces
$1/2$ red chilli, seeded and finely sliced
1 slice of ginger, 2 mm ($1/8$ in) thick, cut into fine sticks
1 clove garlic, finely chopped
300 g (10 oz) piece of firm fish fillet, cut into bite-sized strips
juice of $1/4$ lemon
1 tbsp light soy sauce
$1/2$ tsp sesame oil

Place the Chinese broccoli in a bowl and cover with boiling water. Leave for 5 minutes, then drain.

Heat the oil in a wok or non-stick frypan and stir-fry the spring onion, chilli, ginger and garlic for 1 minute. Add the fish and stir-fry until the fish is almost cooked through. Add the drained broccoli and stir well. Add the lemon juice, soy sauce and sesame oil. Stir well and serve.

Garfish and Vegetable Tempura

If you are not
sure if the oil is
hot enough to
cook the fish,
test the oil with a
piece of battered
vegetable first.
Take great care
not to burn
yourself during
the cooking.

A tempura batter is thinner and lighter than a traditional English batter and therefore absorbs less oil during the cooking.

Serves 2–4

approx. 8 finger-sized pieces of vegetables such as snowpeas, capsicum, spring (green) onions, pumpkin

4 small sprigs of flat-leaf parsley

4 medium garfish, gutted and cleaned, with their heads on (or off, if you don't like to see fish heads!)

$1/2$ cup chilled water

1 egg, lightly beaten

$1/2$ cup plain flour

$1/4$ cup cornflour

$3/4$ teaspoon baking powder

salt

2 cups vegetable oil

Prepare the vegetables.

Pat the garfish dry, using kitchen paper.

Place the chilled water and egg in a bowl. Mix well, then gently whisk in the flour, cornflour, baking powder and salt.

Heat oil in a wok or deep fryer. When the oil is hot, dip fish very slowly and carefully into the batter one at a time before frying in hot oil until light golden. Drain on kitchen paper. Cook the vegetable sticks in the same way, cooking the sprigs of parsley last. Drain the vegetables on kitchen paper and serve immediately.

Spaghetti with Seafood

To devein prawns, make a cut about 3 mm-deep along the back of the prawn after shelling it and, using the blade of a small knife, pull the vein away.

I prefer to buy prawns and scallops and other types of seafood individually rather than using the marinara mix that fish shops offer, as it is often watery.

Serves 2

200 g (7 oz) spaghetti or other pasta

2 tbsp olive oil

$1/2$ white onion, finely chopped

6 large green prawns, shelled, deveined and cut in half

8 scallops, cleaned

8 calamari rings

$1/4$ cup dry white wine or 1 tbsp brandy

1 cup Italian-style tomato sauce, bottled or home-made (see page 84)

1 clove garlic, finely chopped

a pinch of cayenne pepper

2 tbsp chopped parsley

salt and freshly ground black pepper

Bring a large saucepan of salted water to the boil and cook the pasta in boiling water until it is al dente.

Meanwhile, heat the oil in a wok or large non-stick pan and stir-fry the onion on a medium heat for 20 seconds. Increase the heat and add the prawns, scallops and calamari and stir-fry for 1 minute. Add the wine and bring to the boil. Add the tomato sauce, bring back to a simmer and reheat. Stir in the garlic, cayenne pepper and parsley and season with salt and pepper. Toss the pasta with the sauce and serve.

Baked Mackerel
the Spanish Way

Mediterraneans love mackerel cooked in dry white wine, olive oil, herbs and tomatoes.

Serves 4

4 tomatoes

2 tbsp olive oil

1 small white onion, sliced

3 sprigs of parsley

1 clove garlic, crushed

4 small mackerel, about 250 g (8 oz) each, or 2 larger ones, cleaned

$1/4$ cup dry white wine

salt and freshly ground black pepper

Preheat the oven to 200°C (400°F).

Halve the tomatoes and squeeze out the seeds and juice. Chop the tomatoes coarsely.

Place a quarter of the oil in a glass or porcelain oven dish just large enough to hold the fish. Scatter the onion in the dish and top with parsley and garlic. Lay the fish on the bed of onion and herbs. Pour the wine over the fish and top with the chopped tomatoes and the remaining oil. Season with salt and pepper.

Cover the dish with foil and bake in the preheated oven for about 20 minutes or until the fish are cooked through.

Baked Red Snapper Cutlets with a Mango Salsa

Naturally, you can use a fish other than snapper, such as barramundi or blue eye. Serve with steamed Asian vegetables of your choice and jasmine rice.

Serves 2

$1/4$ tsp sesame oil

1 tbsp vegetable oil

1 tbsp soy sauce

freshly ground black pepper

2 snapper cutlets, about 180 g (6 oz) each

$1/2$ tbsp fish sauce

juice of $1/2$ lime or 1 tbsp lemon juice

$1/4$ cup diced ripe, fresh mango

2 tbsp coriander leaves

2 spring (green) onions, finely sliced

Preheat the oven to 220°C (425°F).

In a small bowl combine the sesame oil, half the vegetable oil, half the soy sauce and a little pepper to make a marinade.

Place the fish in a suitable oven dish and pour the marinade over the top. Cover the dish with foil and bake the fish in the preheated oven for about 20 minutes or until cooked.

Meanwhile, mix the fish sauce, the remaining soy sauce and oil, lime juice, mango and a little black pepper in a bowl.

Place the cooked fish on a plate, top with the mango salsa and sprinkle with coriander leaves and spring onions.

Baked Snapper with Fennel

What a beautiful fish snapper is, especially when cooked whole!
Adjust the recipe according to the size of the fish you have
bought or caught.

Serves 2

1 snapper, about 750 g (1$\frac{1}{2}$ lb), scaled and cleaned

salt and freshly ground black pepper

2 tbsp olive oil

$\frac{1}{4}$ white onion or 1 shallot, finely chopped

1 tsp fennel seeds

3 sprigs of parsley

$\frac{1}{4}$ cup dry white wine

Preheat the oven to 200°C (400°F).

Make a few 1 cm-deep cuts into the thickest part of the fish on
both sides and season the fish with salt and pepper.

Place half the oil in an oven dish large enough to hold the
snapper. Put half the onion, half the fennel seeds and the parsley
on the base of the dish. Place the fish on top and scatter the
remaining onion and fennel seeds over the fish. Drizzle the wine
and remaining oil over the fish, cover the dish with foil and bake
in the preheated oven for about 25 minutes.

Discard the parsley and serve the fish with the juices.

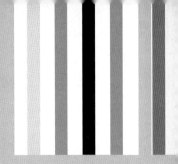

CHICKEN

Chicken is a family meat par excellence. It's affordable and easy to cook, with a delicate flavour and tender texture. Modern poultry shops offer many different varieties and cuts of chicken, ranging from a whole chicken for roasting to boned and skinned chicken thighs for stir-frying. Chicken is a meat for all cuisines, as it marries well with most herbs, spices and condiments. Unlike beef or lamb, chicken *must* be cooked through. A little care needs to be taken when cooking chicken fillets, as they can be dry and not so enjoyable if overcooked. Other cuts, like drumsticks, thighs, wings and winglets are still pleasant when slightly overcooked.

Cooking Times for Chicken

Whole chicken: 1 hour at 180°C (350°F) for a 1.6 kg (3 lb) chicken.   **Roasting**

Chicken leg or 'Maryland' portion (thigh with drumstick attached): about 35 minutes at 180°C (350°F).

Drumstick: about 25–30 minutes at 180°C (350°F).

Boneless fillet: brown first in a frypan for 1 minute on each side, then roast for 10–15 minutes at 180°C (350°F); 5 minutes more for a fillet with the bone.

Wings: about 5 minutes on each side on a medium heat.   **Barbecuing**

Drumstick: about 20 minutes on a medium heat, turning frequently.

Boneless fillet: about 5–7 minutes on each side on a medium heat.

Fillet with the bone: about 8–10 minutes on each side.

Thigh on the bone: about 8 minutes on each side on a medium heat.

Boneless fillet: cook in a little oil in a frying pan on a high heat for   **Pan-frying**
1 minute, then lower the heat and cook a further 3 minutes. Increase the heat, turn the fillet over and cook for 1 minute. Then lower the heat, cover chicken with foil and cook for a further 3 minutes.

Drumstick: about 20 minutes on a medium heat, turning frequently.

Boneless thigh: 4 minutes on each side on a medium heat.

Thigh on the bone: about 6–8 minutes on each side on a medium heat. Cover with foil for the last 3 minutes.

A small quantity of chicken cut into strips takes about 3 minutes.   **Stir-frying**
A larger quantity takes longer.

Chicken on the bone in portions, e.g. drumsticks, thighs, etc. takes   **Casseroling**
about 30–40 minutes in a casserole dish.

Quick Olive and Fetta Chicken

Obviously a Mediterranean-style dish. I like to use chicken thighs for their firm texture and strong flavour. Serve with a green salad.

Serves 2

1 tbsp olive oil

3 boned chicken thighs, each cut into 4 pieces

$1/2$ small brown onion, chopped

$1/4$ cup dry white wine

1 tsp chicken stock powder (optional)

1 cup Italian-style tomato sauce, bottled or home-made (see page 84)

salt and freshly ground black pepper

12 kalamata olives

about 60 g (2 oz) fetta cheese, cubed

2 tbsp chopped parsley

$1/2$ clove garlic, finely chopped

Heat the oil in a wok or medium-sized non-stick frypan and brown the chicken pieces for about 6–8 minutes. Transfer the chicken without the fat to a plate and cover with foil.

Add the onion to the wok and stir-fry on a medium heat without browning for about 3 minutes. Add the wine and stock powder, stir briefly then bring to the boil. Add the tomato sauce, bring back to the boil and season with salt and pepper. Simmer for 2 minutes.

Return the chicken to the pan and add the olives, fetta, parsley and garlic. Stir gently, reheat for a few minutes and serve.

Chicken Pesto with Pasta

Cook the chicken either on the barbecue, on a cast-iron grill on top of the stove or in a non-stick pan. You can marinate it overnight.

Serves 2

3 tbsp olive oil

1 clove garlic, chopped

½ cup basil leaves

2 tbsp pine nuts

½ small red chilli (adjust this to your taste)

2 chicken fillets, skinless

150 g (5 oz) spaghetti or other pasta

salt and freshly ground black pepper

2 tbsp parmesan cheese

In a small food processor, blend the oil, garlic, basil, pine nuts and chilli. Transfer half this pesto to a small bowl, cover and refrigerate.

Cut each chicken fillet into four strips. Toss the strips in the remaining pesto and leave to marinate for 1 hour in the refrigerator.

Cook the pasta in a large pot of salted boiling water until al dente. Drain the pasta.

Meanwhile, barbecue or grill the chicken on a medium heat for about 5 minutes on each side. Season with salt and pepper and cut the chicken into thin slices.

Toss the chicken slices with the pasta, the remaining pesto and season with salt and pepper to taste. Sprinkle with parmesan cheese and serve.

PESTO VARIATIONS

This very flavoursome seasoning goes well with pasta. Simply add a tablespoon of pesto per person to plain pasta. Pesto is also superb on grilled vegetables, fish, lamb or beef.

If basil is out of season, you can use coriander or parsley, and replace the pine nuts with walnuts, macadamia nuts or peanuts. Replace the olive oil with walnut oil. Experiment and have fun!

Stir-fried Chicken with Vegetables

Choose your favourite vegetables for this dish and cut them into regular pieces, remembering that some, such as carrots, are harder and will take longer to cook.

Serves 2

about 250 g (8 oz) boned, skinless chicken pieces

1 tbsp salt-reduced soy sauce

juice of $1/2$ lemon

1 tsp cornflour

about 2 cups green or other vegetables, cut into bite-sized pieces

1 tbsp vegetable oil

$1/2$ clove garlic, chopped

about 1 cup bean sprouts, cleaned

freshly ground black pepper

Cut the chicken into bite-sized strips, place in a bowl with the soy sauce, lemon juice and cornflour and mix together well.

Place the vegetables in a bowl and cover with boiling water. Drain after 5 minutes.

Heat the oil in a wok. Stir in the garlic and chicken pieces and stir-fry on a high heat for just a few minutes until the chicken changes colour. Transfer the chicken pieces to a plate.

Add the vegetables to the wok and stir-fry for about 20 seconds. Add about 2 tablespoons of water down the side of the wok, then cover with a lid and cook for 2–3 minutes until the vegetables are tender, stirring a couple of times.

Add the bean sprouts and chicken pieces and season with pepper and a little extra soy sauce if you wish. Stir well to reheat, and serve.

Stir-fried Chicken with Rice and Peas

A dish that appeals to the younger generation, who love rice and stir-fried food.

Serves 2

1 tbsp olive oil

10 cumin seeds

$1/4$ tsp ground turmeric

$1/2$ cup basmati or jasmine rice

salt and freshly ground black pepper

$1^1/2$ cups boiling water

400 g (14 oz) peas, shelled

2 thin slices of ginger

300 g (10 oz) chicken thigh fillets, cut into bite-sized pieces

$1/2$ small brown onion, finely chopped

$1/2$ clove garlic, chopped

3 drops sesame oil

1 tbsp soy sauce

2 tbsp finely sliced coriander leaves

Heat half the oil in a saucepan. Stir in the cumin seeds and turmeric, then add the rice and stir on a medium heat for 30 seconds. Season with salt and pepper, then add $1^1/2$ cups boiling water and the peas. Cover with a lid, lower the heat and cook for 12 minutes or until all the liquid is absorbed. (Test that the rice is cooked. If not, add a small amount of boiling water and cook a little longer.) Turn off the heat and allow to rest, covered, for 5 minutes before using.

Heat the remaining oil in a wok. Add the ginger and chicken and brown the meat on a high heat. Add the onion and garlic and stir-fry for 5 minutes. Add the sesame oil and soy sauce and season with salt and pepper. Mix in the rice, peas and coriander leaves and serve.

Tandoori-style Chicken

It's fun preparing this dish and once you have understood it,
you'll enjoy creating your own spice mixture for a taste variation,
for example, add chilli for heat, tumeric for colour, extra cumin
for aromatic flavours. Cook the chicken in a very hot oven and
keep an eye on it during the cooking so that it doesn't burn.

Serves 2

1 tbsp Greek-style yoghurt

juice of $1/4$ lemon

$1/2$ tbsp finely grated ginger

$1/2$ clove garlic, finely chopped

1 tsp ground sweet paprika

$1/2$ tsp cumin seeds

1 tsp mild curry powder

a pinch of salt

about $1/4$ tsp freshly ground black pepper

2 skinless chicken Maryland portions (thigh and drumstick)

In a small bowl, thoroughly combine the yoghurt, lemon juice,
ginger, garlic, paprika, cumin seeds, curry powder, salt and
pepper.

Make a few cuts about $1/2$ cm ($1/4$ in) deep here and there into the
chicken flesh, then rub the spicy yoghurt mixture all over the
chicken. Place the chicken on a plate and leave to marinate in the
refrigerator for 1–4 hours.

Preheat the oven to 250°C (475°F).

Place the chicken pieces on an oven rack resting on an oven tray
lined with foil. Bake the chicken in the preheated oven then,
after 15 minutes, turn the pieces over and cook for a further
15 minutes or until the chicken is ready.

Serve with steamed rice (for method see absorption cooking,
page 91).

Pan-fried Chicken Fillets with Lemon and Oregano

This very simple dish has the enticing flavour of lemon and oregano. Avoid overcooking the chicken, and if you're unsure whether the chicken is cooked, cut a piece in half to check it. This dish is delicious served with mashed potato.

Serves 2

2 medium-sized chicken fillets, skinless
a little plain flour to coat the chicken
salt and freshly ground black pepper
1 tbsp olive oil
juice of 1 lemon
about 1 tsp dried oregano

Coat the chicken fillets lightly with plain flour and season with salt and pepper.

Heat the oil in a small, non-stick pan on a high heat and cook the fillets for about 1 minute. Reduce the heat to medium and cook the chicken for a further 2–3 minutes. Turn the fillets over and increase the heat for 1 minute, then lower the heat slightly and cook for a further 2–3 minutes.

Add the lemon juice and oregano to the pan and shake the pan. Turn the heat off, cover chicken with foil and leave for 2 minutes before serving.

Skinless Tex-Mex Roast Chicken

This flavoursome recipe makes an appetising, nicely browned skinless roast. Use more or fewer spices, depending on your taste but don't make it too hot – you can always serve some chilli paste on the side. If you wish, use a poussin (small chicken) which serves 2.

Serves 4

1 chicken, preferably free-range, about 1.2 kg (2½ lb)
2 tbsp olive oil
1 large clove garlic, finely chopped
juice of ½ lemon or lime
2 tsp ground coriander
2 tsp ground cumin
½ tsp ground cinnamon
¼ tsp ground chilli
½ tsp freshly ground black pepper
1 tsp cornflour
1 tsp tomato paste (optional)

Cut the chicken in half using a large knife or poultry scissors. Skin the chicken and trim off any visible fat.

In a bowl, combine the oil, garlic, lemon juice, coriander, cumin, cinnamon, chilli, pepper, cornflour and tomato paste. Brush the chicken all over with this seasoning and, if you have time, marinate for 1 hour.

Preheat the oven to 200°C (400°F).

Line a roasting tray with a sheet of foil and place a roasting rack on top. Sit the chicken on the rack and roast in the preheated oven for about 40 minutes. Reduce the temperature to 160°C (325°F) after a while if the chicken is browning too quickly.

Remove the chicken from the oven, cover with foil and leave to rest for 5 minutes before portioning and serving it.

Baked Cajun Chicken with Onion and Potatoes

At almost all supermarkets you'll find a Cajun spice mix, which is aromatic but not too hot. It is usually made up of dried oregano, thyme, onion powder, garlic powder, cayenne pepper, paprika and a few other spices.

Serves 4

2 tbsp olive oil

1 tbsp Cajun spice mix

8 small chicken drumsticks

4 medium potatoes, peeled and diced

1 small brown onion, diced

$1/2$ tbsp rosemary leaves

salt and freshly ground black pepper

Preheat the oven to 200°C (400°F).

In a bowl mix half the olive oil with the Cajun spice mix. Skin the chicken pieces and toss them in this preparation.

Heat a baking dish, preferably non-stick, then add the remaining oil. Brown the chicken pieces on a high heat for a few minutes. Add the potatoes, onion and rosemary, toss well and cook for 3–4 minutes. Season with salt and pepper.

Place the baking dish in the preheated oven and bake for about 20 minutes or until the chicken and potatoes are cooked.

Serve with a green salad.

Chicken Provençal with Olives

FREE-RANGE CHICKENS

Free-range chickens are more expensive but tastier than battery chickens. The extra flavour comes from the increased exercise they get and sometimes from the food the free-range chickens eat. On the other hand, battery chickens are usually more tender than free-range chickens. If you want chemical-free chickens, buy organic.

I see this as a weekend dish – not that it's difficult to prepare, but it has a gourmet touch. If possible, use free-range chicken and serve with peas, sautéed mushrooms or vegetables of your choice.

Serves 4

4 large tomatoes

1 tbsp olive oil

4 chicken drumsticks, skinless

4 chicken thighs, skinless

1 small brown onion, chopped

2 sprigs of thyme, chopped

$1/4$ cup dry white wine

1 clove garlic, crushed

salt and freshly ground black pepper

$1/2$ cup small kalamata olives

$1/2$ cup basil leaves, finely sliced

Remove the eyes of the tomatoes. Halve the tomatoes and squeeze out the seeds and juice, then chop the tomatoes or cut them into small dice.

Heat the oil in a wide non-stick frypan or in a wok. Brown the chicken for 2–3 minutes. Add the onion and thyme and stir for another 2–3 minutes. Add the wine, bring to the boil and boil for 30 seconds. Add the tomatoes and garlic and stir well. Season with salt and pepper and bring to a simmer. Cover with foil and a lid and cook at a simmer for 20–25 minutes or until the chicken is cooked.

Stir in the olives and reheat for 2 minutes. Just before serving, stir in the freshly cut basil leaves.

Chicken and Capsicum Casserole

Serves 2

4 skinless chicken pieces on the bone, e.g. 2 thighs, 2 drumsticks
1 tbsp cornflour
salt and freshly ground black pepper
1 tbsp olive oil
$\frac{1}{2}$ red chilli
1 large red capsicum, cut into bite-sized pieces
$\frac{1}{4}$ cup dry white wine or water or 1 tbsp dry sherry
$\frac{1}{2}$ cup chicken stock (see page 40)
12 pitted black olives
2 tbsp chopped parsley
$\frac{1}{2}$ clove garlic, finely chopped

Dust the chicken pieces with cornflour and season with salt and pepper.

Heat the oil in a large non-stick saucepan and brown the chicken on all sides for a few minutes.

Stir in the chilli and capsicum and stir for 2 minutes. Add the wine and bring to the boil. Add the stock and bring to a simmer. Cover with foil and a lid and cook on a low heat for 20 minutes.

Stir in the olives and reheat for 1 minute. Stir in the parsley and garlic and serve.

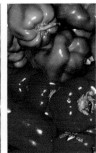

Chicken, Prune and Bacon Casserole

Skinless, free-range chicken thighs and drumsticks would be my favourite cut for this flavoursome casserole.

Serves 2

1 tbsp olive oil
$1/2$ small brown onion, diced
100 g ($3^1/2$ oz) bacon, cut into fine strips
4 skinless chicken pieces on the bone
salt and freshly ground black pepper
2 tsp chopped thyme
about $1/2$ tbsp plain flour
$1/4$ cup red wine
1 small clove garlic, crushed
$3/4$ cup chicken stock (see page 40)
1 large carrot, diced
12 pitted prunes
2 tbsp chopped parsley

Preheat the oven to 180°C (350°F).

Heat the oil in a wide flameproof casserole dish on the stove top and brown the onion, bacon and chicken pieces for 3–4 minutes. Season with salt and pepper and add the thyme. Sprinkle flour over the meat and stir well.

Add the wine and garlic then bring to the boil and boil for 10 seconds. Add the stock and stir well. Add the carrots and prunes and bring to a simmer. Cover with foil and a lid and bake in the preheated oven for about 30 minutes.

Transfer the chicken, carrots and prunes to a deep serving dish and cover with foil.

Bring the liquid in the casserole dish to the boil and stir well. Cook on a high heat to reduce the liquid to a sauce consistency.

Pour the hot sauce over the chicken, carrots and prunes in the serving dish. Sprinkle with chopped parsley and serve.

Easy Family Chicken Curry

Most curries start with a mixture of chopped onion, garlic and ginger. This can be prepared in a food processor to save time and effort.

Serves 4

2 cm (1 in) piece of fresh ginger

1 tbsp vegetable oil

1 tsp fennel seeds

½ brown onion, finely chopped

2 cloves garlic, finely chopped

1 tbsp curry powder

6 boned medium-sized chicken thigh fillets, halved

400 g (14 oz) can diced tomatoes

salt and freshly ground black pepper

1 tsp ground cumin

juice of ½ lemon

3 tbsp finely sliced coriander leaves

Peel then finely slice and chop the ginger.

Heat the wok and add the oil. Stir in the fennel seeds, onion, garlic and ginger and cook on a low to medium heat without browning for 3–4 minutes.

Add the curry powder and stir well, then add the chicken thigh fillets and stir for 2 minutes. Add the tomatoes, stir well and season with salt and pepper. Bring to a simmer, cover and cook for 10 minutes.

Stir in the cumin, lemon juice and coriander leaves and serve.

Grilled Chicken and Salad Burritos

Burritos are a Mexican dish made with tortillas (flat pancakes) and a tasty filling of meat and salad. Tortillas (also labelled 'burritos') are available at supermarkets and are made using wheat or cornmeal.

Serves 2

250 g (8 oz) chicken meat from the breast or thigh, skinless and boneless

$1/2$ tbsp olive oil

$1/4$ tsp ground cumin

$1/2$ small clove garlic, finely chopped

$1/4$ tsp ground coriander

$1/2$ tsp tomato paste

a pinch of chilli powder

salt and freshly ground black pepper

2 tortillas

1 cup shredded cos lettuce

$1/4$ red onion, finely sliced

2 tbsp diced cucumber

$1/4$ avocado, diced

1 small tomato, diced

Cut the chicken into six pieces and place in a bowl with the oil, cumin, garlic, coriander, tomato paste and chilli powder. Toss well and marinate in the refrigerator for 30 minutes if you have time.

Cook the chicken either on a grill plate, under a hot grill or in a non-stick pan or wok for 3–4 minutes on each side. Season with salt and pepper.

Place the tortillas on plates. Garnish with lettuce, onion, cucumber, avocado, tomato and the chicken pieces. Roll up tightly and eat straight away.

Spicy Chicken with Peas and Peanuts

Make this delicious light curry in a wok or large non-stick saucepan, and add vegetables such as mushrooms and cauliflower.

Serves 4

1 tbsp peanut oil

$1/2$ brown onion, chopped

1 clove garlic, chopped

$1/2$ tbsp finely grated ginger

$1/2$ tsp aniseed

$1/2$ tsp mustard seeds

$1/2$ tsp cumin seeds

2 tsp curry powder

8 chicken pieces on the bone, e.g. drumsticks, thighs

$1^1/2$ cups plain yoghurt mixed with 1 tbsp cornflour

salt and freshly ground black pepper

2 cups cooked peas

2 tbsp raw peanuts

2 tbsp sultanas

3 tbsp finely sliced coriander leaves

Heat the oil in a wok and cook the onion, garlic and ginger on a medium heat for about 3 minutes. Stir in the aniseed, mustard, cumin seeds, then the curry powder.

Add the chicken pieces and stir well for 3 minutes. Stir in the yoghurt and season with a little salt and pepper. Bring to a simmer, cover with a lid and cook for 20–30 minutes.

Stir in the peas, peanuts and sultanas and reheat. Just before serving, stir in the coriander.

Spicy Roast Duck Legs

Many poultry shops and supermarkets now sell duck in portions, either fillets or legs. The legs are great value for money, costing about the same as chicken fillets.

Serves 2

2 duck legs
1 tsp coriander seeds
$1/4$ tsp fennel seeds
$1/4$ tsp cumin seeds
1 tsp sea salt
$1/2$ tbsp olive oil

Preheat the oven grill.

Trim off the excess fat from around the duck legs.

Using a mortar and pestle or the base of a saucepan against a chopping board, crush the coriander seeds so they each break into two or three pieces.

In a small bowl, combine crushed coriander seeds with the fennel and cumin seeds, sea salt and olive oil. Rub the skin side of the duck legs with this spicy mix.

Line a roasting tray with foil and sit a roasting rack in the tray. Place the duck legs, skin-side up, on the rack and position the tray so that the meat is about 10 cm (4 in) from the grill. Cook the duck legs for about 5 minutes, making sure they do not burn.

Turn off the grill and continue cooking in a hot oven at 220°C (425°F) for about 25 minutes. During the cooking, the fat will melt and fall into the tray and the duck will become very tender.

Serve with plenty of green vegetables or a mixed salad.

If you do not have an internal grill, cook the duck in the oven at 220°C (425°F) for 30 minutes, making sure it does not burn.

MEAT

I live in Melbourne where the quality of meat is mostly excellent all year round and it's the same for most of Australia. It's worthwhile mastering the technique of cooking a steak, a roast, a meat stir-fry and a meat casserole. Get to know a good butcher who communicates well and you'll learn from him. Most health experts agree that, when trimmed of fat and eaten in moderation, meat is an excellent source of protein, iron, minerals and B vitamins. For many it is also a very satisfying, delicious food which can be the star of the meal.

Stir-frying Meat

Ask your butcher's advice on the best cut of meat to use. Rump steak is often favoured for stir-frying in Asian dishes.

Trim the meat of all fat and gristle before cutting it against the grain into long, regular, thin strips about 5 cm (2 in) long, 2.5 cm (1 in) wide and 5 mm (¼ in) thick.

Mix meat with marinade. The marinade will vary depending on the dish, but soy sauce, dry sherry or rice wine, and cornflour are common ingredients.

To stir-fry, heat a little oil in a hot wok. Swirl the hot oil around the pan, then add the meat and stir-fry until it changes colour. Pork and chicken take a little longer than beef to cook. It is best to stir-fry only about 250–300 g (8–10 oz) meat at a time. A larger quantity cools the wok too much and stews rather than browns.

Pre-cooked vegetables can be added to the browned meat and reheated together.

Using Meat in Casseroles
(osso buco, curries, beef burgundy, etc.)

Tell your butcher which dish you are preparing. Favourite casserole cuts are: shin, chuck, blade and other cuts. If you buy gravy beef, check that it does not have too much gristle, skin and fat.

Remove any excess fat and gristle. Cut the meat into regular pieces or cubes.

If the recipe calls for you to brown the meat, use a non-stick pan and a minimum of fat. You can coat the meat in flour or cornflour if you wish to have a thicker sauce.

Add any liquid in the recipe to the meat once it has browned. This is also a good time to add seasoning. During the cooking, juices released by the meat will mix with the cooking liquid, so it is best not to cover the meat with too much liquid to begin with.

Bring the casserole to a very slow simmer, then reduce the heat to keep it simmering. If it boils too quickly, the meat will become dryer. For more efficient cooking cover the meat with foil and a lid.

A casserole cooks well in a low oven at 150°C (300°F). A beef or lamb casserole will take 1½–2 hours to cook well. A chicken casserole will take about 40 minutes when the pieces have bones, or less when the pieces are boned.

Roasting Meat

Select an evenly shaped piece of meat. Trim the meat of excess fat.

If you are roasting a rolled or uneven piece of meat, tie it up with kitchen string to keep it firm, and give it an even shape. This will help it to cook more evenly.

Preheat the oven for about 15 minutes at 220°C (425°F) before roasting.

Brown the roast on all sides on top of the stove in the roasting tray (use a little olive oil). This caramelises the outer part of the roast and gives it a little sweetness. Some people argue that it also seals in the juices. Place the browned roast on a rack in the roasting tray, then put it in the preheated oven. After 5 minutes, reduce the temperature to 150°C (300°F).

If you are roasting a very large roast, e.g. more than 2 kg (4 lb), you may omit the browning before roasting. In that case, put the meat straight into the preheated oven in the roasting tray, then after 5 minutes reduce the temperature to 150°C (300°F). During the cooking, turn the roast over and baste it with the cooking juices in the tray.

A meat thermometer, available at cookware shops, is useful in assessing the degree to which your meat is cooked. When the roast is cooked, remove it from the oven, cover with foil to keep it warm, and rest it before carving for 5 minutes (for a small roast for two people) up to 20 minutes (for a large roast). During the resting stage, the juices that have accumulated towards the centre of the meat, slowly seep back towards the outside, making the meat more tender.

Cooking times for roasting meat

Beef: about 10–20 minutes per 500 g (1 lb) to roast, depending on the desired degree of cooking.

Lamb: 15–25 minutes per 500 g (1 lb), depending on the desired degree of cooking.

Veal: 20–25 minutes per 500 g (1 lb) to be cooked through.

Pork: about 25 minutes per 500 g (1 lb) to be well done.

Popular Beef Cuts and Their Uses

 Eye fillet is very tender but not very flavoursome – it is great for steaks, roasts, delicate stir-fries, shaslicks.

 Sirloin or Porterhouse has a good balance of tenderness and flavour – it is good for steaks, stir-fries, shaslicks, roasts.

 Scotch fillet is tender and flavoursome – ideal for roasting and grilling.

 Rump steak is very tasty and moderately tender – it is good for grilling, steaks, shaslicks, mince, stir-fries.

 Chuck and gravy beef are tasty but need long cooking to become tender – use them in soups, stews, curries, casseroles.

 Blade is tasty but needs moisture to become tender – it is best for braising and pot-roasting.

 Rib roast has an excellent balance of flavour and tenderness – best for roasting and grilling.

 Silverside although tasty needs long cooking – it is usually used for corned beef and braising.

 Shin is very tasty but needs long cooking – use in stews, curries and osso buco.

Hamburgers Home-Style

To keep a hamburger made with lean meat juicy and tender, it is
important not to overcook it. Minced rump steak offers the best
balance of flavour and tenderness in a burger. In this basic recipe
you can flavour your burgers with the herbs and spices of your
choice.

Serves 2

200–250 g (7–9 oz) fresh minced rump steak or other mince
1 tbsp very finely chopped onion
salt and freshly ground black pepper
1 tbsp cold water
2 bread rolls
1 tbsp olive oil
$1/2$ medium-sized carrot, peeled and grated
4 slices cooked beetroot
tomato sauce or mustard
4 lettuce leaves
1 medium-sized tomato, finely sliced

In a bowl mix the minced beef, onion, a little salt and pepper
and water until they are just combined. Form into two balls and
flatten them slightly.

Heat the oil in a non-stick pan and cook the burgers for
3–5 minutes on each side.

Halve the bread rolls and toast them, if you wish.

Place a little grated carrot and two slices of beetroot on each
half-roll. Add the cooked meat and perhaps a little sauce. Top
with lettuce and tomato, then replace the top half of the roll.
Serve immediately.

Pan-fried Steak with a Mushroom, Spring Onion and Green Peppercorn Sauce

Serves 2

about 150 g (5 oz) green beans
1 tbsp oil
2 sirloin steaks, 2 cm (1 in) thick, trimmed of fat
salt and freshly ground black pepper
1 cup diced mushrooms
1 tsp beef stock powder
$1/2$ cup boiling water
1 tsp cornflour mixed with 2 tbsp white or red wine
3 spring (green) onions, cut into 3 cm (1 in) pieces
2 tsp green peppercorns

Top and tail the beans and cut them into 2 cm ($3/4$ in) pieces. Cook the beans in salted boiling water, then drain.

Heat the oil in a frying pan and cook the steaks for about 2 minutes on each side. Transfer the steaks to plates, season with salt and pepper and keep warm.

Add the mushroom and stock powder to the pan and stir for 1 minute. Add the boiling water, return to the boil and stir in the cornflour mixture until the sauce thickens. Add the beans, spring onions and peppercorns. Reheat and season to taste with salt and pepper. Spoon the sauce over the steaks and serve immediately.

Rump Steak Kebabs

Rump is an ideal beef cut for kebabs, as it offers a good balance of flavour and tenderness. Marinate the meat for 2–24 hours. Soak eight bamboo sticks in water for 30 minutes before threading the meat onto them.

Makes 8 kebabs

about 700 g (1$\frac{1}{2}$ lb) rump steak, about 3 cm (1 in) thick
1 tbsp finely chopped thyme
1 tsp cracked or freshly ground black pepper
$\frac{1}{2}$ tsp ground sweet paprika
$\frac{1}{2}$ tsp chilli paste (optional)
2 tbsp olive oil
1 clove garlic, very finely chopped
2 red or green capsicums
salt

Cut the meat into 3 cm (1 in) cubes, trimming off as much fat as possible.

In a bowl, combine the thyme, pepper, paprika, chilli paste, olive oil and garlic. Add the meat and toss well. Cover and refrigerate for at least 2 hours.

Halve the capsicums, remove the seeds and cut into about 3 cm (1 in) squares.

Thread the pieces of meat and capsicum onto the soaked bamboo sticks. Cook on a hot barbecue, in a non-stick frying pan or under the grill for 3–4 minutes on each side, turning them halfway through the cooking.

Season with a little salt just before serving with an assortment of salads.

Cooking steak about 3 cm (1 in) thick

Rare

Cook on a high heat for about 2 minutes on each side. The meat should be brown on both sides but very soft to the touch. The centre of the meat will still be raw.

Medium-rare

Cook on a high heat for about 3 minutes on each side. Turn the heat off and rest the meat for 1 minute before serving. The meat will offer little resistance to the touch and the centre will still be very pink.

Medium

Cook on a medium to high heat for about 4 minutes on each side. Turn the heat off and rest the meat for 1 minute before serving. The meat will offer resistance to the touch but should not be dry. The centre will be pink turning grey.

Well-done

Cook on a medium to high heat for about 5 minutes on each side. Turn the heat off and rest the meat for 1 minute before serving. The meat will not be flexible to the touch and will be cooked through. The colour at the centre will be greyish with a little moisture.

Peppered Steak with a Tomato and Olive Salsa

Sirloin and rump are two excellent cuts for this easy-to-prepare dish. Avoid overcooking the meat.

Serves 2

1 tsp cracked black pepper
2 steaks, about 2.5 cm (1 in) thick
1 large tomato
2 tbsp chopped parsley
8 kalamata olives, pitted and sliced
$1/2$ clove garlic, finely chopped
salt and freshly ground black pepper
1 tbsp olive oil

Sprinkle the pepper over the steaks.

Cut the tomato into 1 cm ($1/2$ in) dice. Place in a bowl and mix with the parsley, olives and garlic. Season with salt and pepper and add half the olive oil.

Heat the remaining oil in a frying pan. When hot, cook the steaks for 2–4 minutes on each side, depending on how you like them done. When the steaks are ready, season them with a little salt and pepper, then transfer them to plates. Spoon the salsa over the meat and serve immediately.

Stir-fried Beef with Green Vegetables

It's great to learn to stir-fry dishes of meat and vegetables. If you find cooking three different vegetables too much of a challenge, try doing it with just one vegetable, such as snow peas.

Serves 2

200 g (7 oz) lean rump steak
$1/2$ tbsp soy sauce
$1/2$ tbsp dry sherry
1 tsp cornflour
100 g ($3^1/2$ oz) French beans
100 g ($3^1/2$ oz) snow peas
1 cup broccoli florets
1 tbsp peanut or polyunsaturated vegetable oil
$1/2$ clove garlic, crushed
2 thin slices ginger
2 tbsp water
1 tbsp roasted blanched almonds
$1/2$ tsp hot chilli paste (optional)

Trim the beef of all fat and cut into bite-sized strips. In a bowl, mix the beef with the soy sauce, sherry and cornflour.

Bring a large saucepan of water to the boil. Wash, top and tail the beans and snow peas. Drop the beans and broccoli into the saucepan and boil for 2 minutes. Drain.

Place the snow peas in a bowl and cover with boiling water. Leave for 2 minutes, then drain.

Heat half the oil in a wok. Add the garlic, ginger and beef and stir-fry until the meat has browned. Transfer the meat to a plate and discard the ginger.

Add the remaining oil into the wok and stir-fry the beans and broccoli for about 15 seconds, before pouring the 2 tablespoons of water down the side of the wok. Stir well, cover the wok and cook until the vegetables are tender but still slightly crunchy. Add the beef, almonds and snow peas, stir well and reheat. Serve chilli paste separately.

Stir-fried Curried Beef and Cauliflower

Served on a bed of plain rice, this quick dish offers lovely flavours. Try using broccoli, beans or zucchini instead of cauliflower.

Serves 2

2 cups cauliflower florets
1 tbsp vegetable oil
about 300 g (10 oz) cubed rump or sirloin
$\frac{1}{2}$ onion, chopped
1 small clove garlic, chopped
1 tsp curry powder
$\frac{1}{2}$ tsp turmeric
1 tsp peanut butter
1 tbsp dry sherry or white wine
$\frac{1}{2}$ tbsp soy sauce
salt and freshly ground black pepper
3 spring onions, cut into small pieces

Cook the cauliflower in salted boiling water until just soft, then drain.

Heat the oil in a wok or non-stick frypan and stir-fry the beef cubes until browned all over. Transfer the beef to a plate.

Add the onion and garlic to the wok and stir-fry on a low heat for 3 minutes. Stir in the curry powder, turmeric, peanut butter and sherry.

Return the meat to the pan and toss well. Add the soy sauce and cauliflower and season with salt and pepper. Stir-fry to reheat well, scatter the spring onions on top and serve.

Curried Meatballs

Enjoy these spicy meatballs with basmati rice, Asian noodles
or mashed potato.

Serves 4

1 tbsp vegetable oil
1 medium brown onion, finely chopped
$1/4$ cup cold water
1 tsp ground cumin
$1/2$ tsp chilli paste
600 g ($1 1/4$ lb) lean minced beef
$1/2$ cup finely chopped coriander leaves
salt and freshly ground black pepper
2 cloves garlic, finely chopped
$1/2$ tbsp grated ginger
$1/4$ tsp coriander seeds
$1/4$ tsp mustard seeds
$1/2$ tsp cumin seeds
1 tbsp curry powder
400 g (14 oz) can diced tomatoes

Heat the oil in a wide non-stick pan or frypan and cook the
onion on a medium heat for 3 minutes. Turn off the heat and
transfer half the onion to a large mixing bowl.

Add the water, ground cumin and chilli paste to the bowl. When
the onion in the bowl is cold, add the minced beef and half the
chopped coriander. Season with salt and pepper and mix well.
Shape into about twelve meatballs of even size.

Add the garlic, ginger, coriander seeds, mustard seeds and cumin
seeds to the onion in the pan and cook on a medium heat for
2 minutes. Add the curry powder and stir for 10 seconds.

Gently place the meatballs in the pan and brown all over for a
few minutes. Add the diced tomatoes, shake the pan and bring
to a simmer. Cover and cook for 10 minutes.

Just before serving, stir in the remaining coriander leaves.

Chilli con Carne

This dish can be made in advance and in larger quantities which can be frozen then reheated as you need it.

Serves about 8

1 kg (2 lb) lean round steak, casserole beef or coarse minced beef
3 tbsp olive oil
1 large brown onion, chopped
2 large cloves garlic, crushed
1/2 tsp chilli powder or to taste
1 tbsp ground cumin
2 tsp dried oregano
1 tbsp ground sweet paprika
800 g (28 oz) can crushed tomatoes
1 large bay leaf, fresh or dried
1 tsp salt
freshly ground black pepper
2 x 400 g (14 oz) cans kidney beans

Preheat the oven to 180°C (350°F).

Trim the beef of fat and tendons and cut into 1 cm (1/2 in) cubes.

On the stove top, heat a quarter of the oil in a flameproof dish then brown half the meat on a high heat for a few minutes. Transfer the meat to a bowl. Heat another quarter of the oil. Brown the remaining meat and transfer to the bowl.

Add the remaining oil to the dish. Add the onion and stir-fry for 3 minutes. Stir in the garlic, chilli, cumin, oregano and paprika. Add the tomatoes and bay leaf and season with salt and pepper. Stir in the meat, cover the dish with foil and a lid, and cook in the preheated oven for about 1 1/2 hours.

Remove from the oven and stir in the drained kidney beans. Reheat on low heat for about 5 minutes.

Serve with tortillas, nachos or some good bread.

Beef Shaslicks with Macadamia Pesto

Serves 2

a slice of rump steak, about 300 g (10 oz), 3 cm (1 in) thick
6 macadamia nuts
1 clove garlic, peeled
about 20 basil leaves
2 tbsp olive oil
freshly ground black pepper
salt

Soak four bamboo sticks in cold water for about an hour.

Trim off all visible fat and cut the meat into regular cubes. Place in a bowl.

In a small blender, process the macadamia nuts, garlic, basil leaves, oil and a little pepper into a purée. Mix this purée with the beef cubes and marinate in the refrigerator for at least 30 minutes.

Thread the marinated meat cubes onto bamboo sticks. Refrigerate if you are not using them immediately.

Cook the shaslicks on a high heat in a lightly oiled, non-stick pan or on a grill plate for a few minutes on each side. Season with salt.

Serve with a mixed salad and mashed potato.

Meatballs Italian-style

You can adapt
this dish to your
taste by varying
the seasoning of
herbs, for
example, use
basil, tarragon or
coriander instead
of parsley. Serve
it with pasta and a
mixed vegetable
salad.

Serves 4

3 tbsp olive oil

1 small brown onion, finely chopped

500 g (1 lb) lean minced beef

1 egg

3 tbsp dry breadcrumbs

4 tbsp chopped parsley

2 tbsp grated parmesan cheese

1 clove garlic, finely chopped

1 tbsp chopped raisins or sultanas

salt and freshly ground black pepper

a little plain flour to coat the meatballs

3 tbsp white wine

400 g (14 oz) can diced tomatoes or 2 cups Italian-style tomato
sauce, bottled or home-made (see page 84)

Heat 1 tablespoon of the oil in a non-stick frypan and cook the
onion on a medium heat for about 5 minutes without browning
too much. Transfer the onion to a large bowl and allow to cool.

Preheat the oven to 180°C (350°F).

Add the minced meat to the onion and mix well by hand. Add
the egg, breadcrumbs, half the parsley, parmesan, garlic and
raisins and season with salt and pepper. Mix very well. Using wet
hands, form the mixture into balls the size of walnuts, then
lightly coat the meatballs with flour.

Heat the remaining oil in a non-stick frypan and brown the
meatballs on all sides.

Transfer the meatballs to an oven dish just large enough to hold
them. Add the wine to the frypan and bring to the boil. Add the
diced tomato to the pan, return to a simmer and stir in the
remaining parsley. Spoon the sauce over the meatballs in the dish
and bake in the preheated oven for 15–20 minutes.

Alternatively, you can cook the meatballs on a low heat on top of
the stove in a covered frypan.

Koftas (Middle Eastern Meatballs)

Enjoy these tasty meatballs with a Greek-style salad and perhaps a dip such as hummus (see page 47) or the yoghurt, tahini and mint dip on page 50.

Serves 2

2 tbsp olive oil
½ brown onion, finely chopped
2 tbsp pine nuts
300 g (10 oz) minced beef
1 tbsp water
1 tsp ground cumin
¼ tsp ground cinnamon
½ tsp ground sweet paprika
a pinch of cayenne or chilli powder
salt and freshly ground black pepper
1 tsp finely grated lemon zest
2 tbsp chopped coriander leaves or parsley

Preheat the oven to 250°C (475°F).

Heat half the oil in a non-stick pan and stir-fry the onion for about 3 minutes without browning. Add the pine nuts and stir until lightly browned. Transfer onto kitchen paper to drain and cool.

In a bowl, combine the minced meat, water, cumin, cinnamon, paprika, cayenne and a little salt and pepper.

Place the pine nuts and onion in a bowl with the lemon zest and coriander.

Take a walnut-sized piece of mince and flatten it in the hands to about 5 mm (¼ in) thick. Spoon about 1 teaspoon of the pine nut and onion mixture onto each meatball then, using wet hands, fold the meat over to envelop the contents and form a ball.

Line a baking dish with baking paper. Arrange the koftas in the dish and brush with the remaining oil. Bake in the hot oven for about 20 minutes, turning them at least once during the cooking.

Cooking on the Barbecue

Before cooking, make sure the barbecue is clean and free of rust. Lightly oil the cleaned barbecue.

Preheat the barbecue well before placing food on it. Keep one side of the barbecue hotter for flexibility of cooking.

Remove food from the fridge about 10–15 minutes before cooking and keep it in a cool place indoors.

Trim chops and steak of any excess fat before placing them on the barbecue. Lightly coat the meat, fish and vegetables with oil before cooking. Avoid placing food with excess marinade, oil or honey on the barbecue, as these will make the food burn fast. Avoid cooking over an open flame, as burnt food is carcinogenic.

Once you have put the food on the barbecue, avoid touching it or moving it for a few minutes, unless it is burning. Supervise the cooking at all times.

Turn meat over after a few minutes – the exact time depends on how you like your meat cooked. Even if you like steak well-done, it's sufficient to cook it for 5 minutes on each side. Avoid leaving meat on the barbecue for too long after cooking, as it will become overcooked and dry, and attract insects.

Fish, chicken and some vegetables, such as corn, potatoes and zucchini, can be cooked in foil on the barbecue. Try something different each time you cook on the barbecue.

Introduce children to barbecue cooking, but stay with them at all times.

Keeping the Barbecue Clean

If the barbecue is dirty, heat it, then scrape off any remnants of food using a metal scraper, and clean with a metal brush. The best time to clean the barbecue is a short time after cooking, when the barbecue is cooling down.

Meatloaf

A meatloaf is a great family favourite. This recipe can easily be changed to suit your taste or mood, or according to what you have on hand in the fridge.

Serves 4–6

500 g (1 lb) lean minced beef

250 g (8 oz) minced pork, or sausage meat (which is fattier)

1 cup finely chopped capsicum

1/2 brown onion, chopped

1 egg

1 tsp salt

1 tsp ground cumin

1/4 tsp chilli powder

4 tbsp chopped parsley

freshly ground black pepper

1/2 cup breadcrumbs

3 tbsp water

2 cups Italian-style tomato sauce, bottled or home-made
(see page 84)

Preheat the oven to 180°C (350°F).

Place the minced beef and pork in a large bowl and combine by hand with the capsicum, onion, egg, salt, cumin, chilli, parsley, pepper, breadcrumbs and water until it holds together well.

Shape the mixture into a loaf and place in the centre of a suitably sized oven dish. Pour the tomato sauce over the loaf and bake in the preheated oven for 1 hour, basting every 20 minutes. If the loaf becomes too dry, add 1–2 tablespoons of boiling water.

Family Meat Pie with Peas in Filo

A family meat pie does not need to be too rich. Use very lean mince, include a vegetable, cook the meat in a minimum of fat and use non-stick cookware. Also, use filo pastry because it has less fat than puff or savoury pastry.

Serves 4

2 tbsp olive oil

1 brown onion, chopped

1 medium-sized carrot, chopped

2 tsp oregano or chopped thyme

500 g (1 lb) lean minced beef

1 cup water

1 tbsp tomato paste

salt and freshly ground black pepper

1 tbsp plain flour mixed with 2 tbsp water

2 cups cooked peas

2 tsp Worcestershire sauce

a little olive oil to grease the pie dish

3 sheets filo pastry

Heat half the olive oil in a large, non-stick saucepan.

On a medium heat, add the onion, carrot and oregano or thyme and stir for about 4 minutes. Increase the heat, add the mince and stir until all the meat has changed colour.

Add the water and tomato paste and season with salt and pepper. Bring to a simmer and cook for about 45 minutes.

Stir in the flour and water mixture, the peas and Worcestershire sauce, then simmer for a further 5 minutes. Transfer to a greased pie dish and allow to cool before cooking the pie.

Preheat the oven to 180°C (350°F).

Brush the sheets of filo with a little olive oil. Cut each sheet into three strips then lay the strips over the pie to cover it evenly. Tuck in pastry around the edge of the dish, then make three or four small holes using the tip of a knife.

Bake in the preheated oven until the pie is hot and the pastry golden brown.

Goulash

This classic East European recipe is perfect for those colder days of the year and for when you have a little more time to cook.

Serves 5

about 1 kg (2 lb) casserole beef (shin, neck, oyster blade)

1 tbsp vegetable oil or light olive oil

1 large onion, sliced

1 tbsp ground sweet paprika

2 cloves garlic, crushed

1 tbsp tomato paste

400 g (14 oz) can diced tomatoes

a few sprigs of parsley, 1 small bay leaf and 2 sprigs of thyme, tied together with kitchen string

1 cup beef stock or vegetable stock (see page 41)

salt and freshly ground black pepper

5 medium-sized potatoes

$1/2$ cup boiling water

Preheat the oven to 150°C (300°F).

Trim the fat from the meat and cut the meat into ten regular pieces.

On the stove top, heat the oil in a wide, flameproof casserole dish and brown the meat and onion for 4–5 minutes. Sprinkle the paprika over the meat and stir in. Add the garlic, tomato paste, diced tomato, herbs and stock and stir well. Season with salt and pepper and bring to a simmer. Cover with foil and a lid and cook in the oven for about 2 hours.

After that time, peel the potatoes, halve them lengthwise and add to the beef. Stir in the boiling water, cover and continue cooking in the oven or on top of the stove until the potatoes are cooked.

Fiery Beef Casserole with Coriander and Macadamia Nuts

A tasty dish to prepare during the cooler months of the year. Plan ahead, as it takes over 2 hours to cook. Alternatively, cook it in a pressure cooker for about 45 minutes.

Serves 4–6

1 long green chilli, halved and seeds removed

1 brown onion, peeled

3 cm (1 in) piece of ginger, peeled

2 cloves garlic

2 tbsp vegetable oil

$^1\!/_2$ tsp mustard seeds

1 tsp coriander seeds, crushed

2 tsp mixed spice

2 tsp ground sweet paprika

about 1 kg (2 lb) cubed beef shin, oyster blade or neck

salt and freshly ground black pepper

2 tsp cornflour

$1^1\!/_2$ cups natural yoghurt

1 cup coriander leaves

15 macadamia nuts

Preheat the oven to 150°C (300°F).

In a food processor, blend the chilli, onion, ginger and garlic to a purée.

On the stove top, heat the oil in a flameproof casserole. Add the onion purée and stir on a medium heat for 5 minutes. Add the mustard and coriander seeds and stir for 10 seconds before adding the mixed spice and paprika. Stir, then add the beef and brown it on a high heat for 3–4 minutes.

Mix the cornflour into the yoghurt and add to the beef. Mix well and season with salt and pepper. Bring to a simmer, cover with a close-fitting lid and cook in the oven for about 2 hours or until the meat is tender.

Chop the coriander leaves and cut the macadamia nuts into small pieces. Stir into the casserole, then taste and adjust the seasoning. Serve with rice, mashed potato or pasta.

What to Do with Leftovers

As soon as leftovers are cold, place them in a suitable container, cover with plastic wrap and refrigerate. Use refrigerated leftovers within 48 hours. After that, most leftovers won't be enjoyable.

Alternatively, place leftovers in a freezer bag or suitable container and freeze.

Leftover vegetables, rice and pasta can be reheated in the microwave.
In most cases, you place the food in a microwave dish, add 1–2 tablespoons of water, cover with plastic film or a lid and reheat on high for a minute or more, depending on the quantity and volume of food.

Leftover steak, pan-fried chicken fillet or roast meat can be used in a sandwich, in a salad or antipasto platter, in a pasta sauce, a rice dish, in a stir-fry with vegetables or in a soup or stew. Cut the meat thinly before using it, as it will be easier to reheat quickly.

It is a great idea occasionally to cook double quantities of soup, stew, curry, etc., but remember, most people don't enjoy eating the same meal three times in a row.

Dry Beef Curry

With this no-fuss, home-made curry, try to marinate the meat with the spices for half a day – the result will be tastier and more tender. Serve with rice and peas.

Serves 4

3 tbsp polyunsaturated vegetable oil
1 tsp cumin seeds
1 tbsp curry powder
$1/2$ brown onion, chopped
1 clove garlic, finely chopped
1 tbsp finely grated ginger
500 g (1 lb) cubed casserole beef
1 tbsp cornflour
$1^1/4$ cups natural yoghurt
$1/2$ cup boiling water
salt and freshly ground black pepper
2 tbsp sultanas
4 tbsp finely chopped fresh coriander leaves

In a bowl, mix together 1 tablespoon of the oil, the cumin seeds, curry powder, onion, garlic, ginger and cubed beef. Cover with plastic wrap and marinate for at least 2 hours in the refrigerator.

Preheat the oven to 150°C (300°F).

Whisk the cornflour into the yoghurt.

Heat the remaining oil in a flameproof casserole dish on the stove top and brown the marinated meat for 3 or 4 minutes. Add the boiling water and stir well. Stir in the yoghurt and cornflour mixture and season with a little salt and pepper. Cover with foil and a close-fitting lid and cook in the preheated oven for $1^1/2$ hours.

Remove from the oven and, if necessary, add a little extra hot water to the curry if it appears too dry. Stir in the sultanas and cook for a further 30 minutes in the oven until the meat is tender.

Just before serving, stir in the coriander.

Quick Red Beef Curry
with Green Beans

This Thai-style curry uses red curry paste, available from supermarkets, Asian grocers and some delis. There are many different brands, some better than others, so you may need to try them.

Serves 2

about 300 g (10 oz) sirloin or rump steak

200 g (7 oz) green beans, cut into bite-sized pieces

1 tbsp vegetable oil

about 1 tbsp chopped brown onion

6 medium mushrooms, sliced

1 tbsp red curry paste

$1/4$ cup water

$1/2$ cup coconut cream

salt

2 tbsp coriander leaves, finely sliced

1 tbsp salted or unsalted peanuts

Trim the steak and cut it into long bite-sized pieces.

Steam the beans until just done, then drain.

Heat half the oil in a non-stick frypan and brown the meat for 1 minute. Transfer the meat to a plate.

Add the remaining oil to the pan and stir-fry the onion for 1 minute. Add the mushrooms and cook for 2 minutes before adding the curry paste and water. Mix well, bring to a simmer and stir in the coconut cream. Return to a simmer and stir in the beans. Add the meat and reheat for 1 minute.

Season to taste with salt and serve sprinkled with coriander and peanuts.

Spicy Beef Casserole with Red Peppers

For a tastier and more tender result, marinate the meat for a few hours or overnight. Serve with steamed or mashed potatoes.

Serves 4

3 tbsp olive oil

1/4 tsp ground cloves or 1 whole clove

1 tbsp ground sweet paprika

1 tsp cracked pepper

2 tsp coriander seeds crushed using the back of a spoon

1 tsp black mustard seeds

600 g (1 1/4 lb) cubed casserole beef (oyster blade or shin)

2 red capsicums

1/2 brown onion, sliced

1 cup beef stock

1 tbsp cornflour mixed with 2 tbsp dry white wine

salt

Preheat the oven to 150°C (300°F).

In a bowl, mix together 1 tablespoon of the oil, the cloves, paprika, cracked pepper, coriander and mustard seeds. Add the beef cubes and coat well. Cover with plastic wrap and refrigerate until required.

Wash, halve and seed the capsicums, then cut each half into 3 pieces.

Heat the remaining oil in a flameproof dish on the stove top. Brown the meat for 3 minutes on a high heat. Add the onion and brown for 2 minutes. Add the beef stock, bring to a simmer, then stir in the cornflour mixture. Season with a little salt and stir well. Add the capsicum and stir again.

Cover with foil and a tight-fitting lid, then cook in the preheated oven for about 2 hours or until tender – check halfway through the time to see that everything is going well.

Veal Rolls in Tomato Sauce

Ask your butcher to tenderise the veal slices for you if it has not already been done. You can also use pork or beef slices. Veal rolls are delicious with pasta or polenta.

Serves 4

4 thin veal slices (the schnitzel cut)
freshly ground black pepper
2 tbsp olive oil
1/2 brown onion, finely chopped
1/2 medium-sized carrot, finely chopped
1 small stick celery, finely chopped
2 sprigs of thyme
2 tbsp dry white wine
400 g (14 oz) can crushed or diced tomatoes
salt
3 tbsp chopped parsley
1 small clove garlic, finely chopped

Preheat oven to 180°C (350°F).

Cut each veal slice into three pieces and season with pepper. Roll each slice up and secure with a toothpick.

On the stove top, heat the oil in a flameproof casserole dish and brown the rolls all over. Transfer them to a plate. Add the onion, carrot, celery and thyme to the casserole dish and cook, stirring, for 3 minutes. Add the wine and bring to the boil, then add the tomatoes. Season with salt and pepper.

Return the meat to the dish. Bring to a simmer, cover with foil and a lid and bake in the preheated oven for 20 minutes.

Stir in the chopped parsley and garlic and serve with the sauce.

Veal Shanks with Lemon and Tomato

For the best
results, you need
well-trimmed veal
shanks with a
fresh-looking,
pink colour, not
too light or too
dark. You may
need to order
them in advance
from your butcher.
It is best to use
a flameproof
casserole dish
that fits the
shanks neatly
at the base.

Serves 2–4

2 tbsp olive oil

2 veal shanks, well-trimmed of skin, fat and tendons

1 small brown onion, diced

1 cup diced celery

1 cup diced carrot

3 sprigs of lemon thyme, finely cut

1 tbsp plain flour

$1/4$ cup dry white wine

1 cup rich beef stock

1 clove garlic, chopped

800 g (28 oz) can diced tomatoes

salt and freshly ground black pepper

juice of $1/2$ lemon

$1/2$ tbsp finely grated lemon zest

2 tbsp chopped parsley

Preheat the oven to 180°C (350°F).

On the stove top, heat the oil in a flameproof casserole dish and brown the veal shanks on all sides for a few minutes. Transfer the shanks to a plate. Add the onion, celery, carrot and thyme to the casserole dish and cook, stirring for 3 to 4 minutes.

Stir in the flour and mix well. Stir in the wine and the stock and bring to a simmer. Return the shanks to the dish with the garlic and place the diced tomato on top. Season with salt and pepper, cover with foil and a lid and cook in the preheated oven for 1 hour.

Turn the shanks over and cook for a further half hour or until the meat is tender.

If the sauce is too runny, remove the meat and boil the sauce down, uncovered, on top of the stove.

Just before serving, stir in the lemon juice, lemon zest and parsley.

Veal Stew with Vegetables

This is a typical French dish where the meat is poached in a liquid rather than browned in oil. It's delicious with steamed rice.

Serves 6

1 kg (2 lb) lean cubed veal, suitable for a casserole or stew

salt and freshly ground white pepper

2 sprigs of thyme

2 sprigs of parsley

1 onion, left whole

2 sticks celery, cut into bite-sized pieces

3 large carrots, peeled and sliced

2 cups shelled peas

1 tbsp cornflour mixed with 2 tbsp dry sherry or water

$1/2$ cup light cream

2 egg yolks

3 tbsp chopped parsley

Place the veal cubes in a large saucepan, just cover with cold water and bring to the boil. When it boils, remove the surface scum, then season with salt and pepper. Add the thyme, parsley and onion, cover the pan and simmer for $1^1/4$ hours or until the meat is almost tender.

Add the carrot, peas and celery to the pan and cook for a further 10 minutes.

Remove the veal and vegetables from the cooking liquid, transferring them to another saucepan. Discard the onion, parsley and thyme.

Bring the cooking liquid to the boil. Stir in the cornflour mixture and mix well. Boil for 2 minutes then lower to a simmer.

Mix the cream and yolks in a bowl, then whisk this into the liquid and immediately add the meat, vegetables and chopped parsley and reheat without boiling.

Serve in bowls.

Veal Stew with Chilli, Lemon and Coriander

This is one of my favourite stews, as I love the delicate texture of the veal and the exciting, combined flavours of chilli, lemon and coriander.

Serves 4

about 800 g (1$\frac{1}{2}$ lb) veal shin, cut into pieces about 5 cm (2 in) square
1 tbsp cornflour
sea salt and freshly ground black pepper
2 tbsp olive oil
1 small onion, finely chopped
1 tbsp finely cut lemon thyme
$\frac{1}{4}$ cup dry white wine
1 cup canned diced tomatoes
1 cup diced celery
2 tsp beef stock powder
1 small red chilli, finely chopped
juice of $\frac{1}{2}$ lemon
1 tbsp finely grated lemon zest
1 cup coriander leaves, chopped

Toss the veal pieces in cornflour and a little salt and pepper.

Heat the oil in a large saucepan or pot. Add the onion and stir on medium heat for 5 minutes. Add the meat and thyme and brown the meat all over. Add the wine, stir well, then add the tomato, celery and stock powder. Mix well, bring to a simmer, cover and cook for about 1$\frac{1}{4}$ hours. If you use a pressure cooker, it will take 20–25 minutes. After this time, check that the meat is tender and cook a little longer if necessary.

Just before serving, add the chilli, lemon juice, lemon zest and coriander and season to taste.

Veal Chops with Capers and Walnuts

Veal chops are tender provided they are not overcooked. When the meat is almost done, turn off the heat and leave the chops to rest and to finish cooking in their own heat. Serve with mashed potato.

Serves 2

1 tbsp olive oil

1 tsp lemon thyme, chopped

$1/2$ tsp cracked pepper

2 veal chops

salt

$1/2$ clove garlic

juice of $1/2$ lemon

1 tsp capers

1 tbsp chopped walnuts

8 finely sliced basil leaves or 1 tbsp chopped parsley or
   15 finely sliced tarragon leaves

On a plate, mix half the olive oil with the lemon thyme and cracked pepper. Rub this mixture all over the chops.

Heat the remaining oil in a non-stick frypan and fry the chops for about 3 minutes on each side. Transfer the chops onto warm plates and season with salt. Cover with foil and allow to rest for 3 minutes.

Place the garlic, lemon juice, capers, walnuts and herbs in the pan. Reheat briefly, then spoon over the veal and serve immediately.

Spicy Veal Sauce

The tastiest veal cut to use is from the shank. Otherwise, use the meat from the shoulder or leg.

Serves 6

$^1/_2$ brown onion

$^1/_2$ medium-sized carrot

1 stick celery

2 tbsp olive oil

600 g (1$^1/_4$ lb)casserole veal, cut into 1.5 cm ($^1/_2$ in) cubes

$^1/_2$ tsp cumin seeds

$^1/_2$ tsp mustard seeds

pinch of cayenne pepper

1 tbsp plain flour

1 tbsp tomato paste

$^1/_4$ cup dry white wine

1 tbsp beef stock powder (optional)

$^1/_2$ cup hot water

400 g (14 oz) can diced or crushed tomatoes

salt and freshly ground black pepper

1 clove garlic, finely chopped

3 tbsp chopped parsley

Preheat the oven to 150°C (300°F).

Chop the onion, carrot and celery either with a knife or in the blender.

Heat half the oil in a flameproof casserole dish on the stove top and brown the meat for a few minutes. Transfer to a bowl.

Add the remaining oil to the dish. Add the cumin, mustard seeds and cayenne pepper and stir-fry for 10 seconds. Add the vegetables and stir-fry for 3 minutes. Return the meat to the pan and stir in the flour, tomato paste and wine. Bring to the boil and add the beef stock, water and diced tomato. Bring to a simmer and season with salt and pepper. Cover the dish with foil and a lid and cook in the preheated oven for about 1$^1/_2$ hours or until the meat is tender. Stir once or twice during the cooking.

Just before serving, stir in the garlic and parsley.

Serve with pasta or baked potatoes.

Rack of Lamb with Brussels Sprout Purée

MEAT

A rack of lamb is a real treat. Choose a well-trimmed, 'frenched' rack or ask your butcher to trim the fat for you. As for the brussels sprout purée, believe me, it is delicious.

Serves 2

a 'trim lamb' frenched rack (7 or 8 chops)
1 tbsp olive oil
1 tbsp finely cut rosemary leaves
$\frac{1}{2}$ clove garlic, finely chopped
freshly ground black pepper
200 g (7 oz) butternut pumpkin
salt
300 g (10 oz) brussels sprouts
$\frac{1}{2}$ cup hot milk
1 tbsp butter or extra olive oil or fat substitute

Preheat the oven to 220°C (425°F). Trim all visible fat from the lamb.

In a small bowl, mix the olive oil with the rosemary, garlic and a little pepper. Rub the meat with this preparation.

Peel the pumpkin then cut the flesh into 1 cm ($\frac{1}{2}$ in) slices. Season with salt and pepper.

Place the lamb in a non-stick roasting tray. Place the pumpkin around the meat and roast in the preheated oven for about 20 minutes, turning the meat and pumpkin at least once during the cooking.

Meanwhile, trim off any damaged brussels sprout leaves then cut a cross 1 cm- ($\frac{1}{2}$ in-) deep into the base of each sprout. Cook the sprouts in salted boiling water until tender.

In a food processor, blend the sprouts with hot milk and butter to a purée, then season with salt and pepper.

Carve the racks into chops, season with salt and pepper and serve with the pumpkin and the sprout purée.

Ground Lamb Kebabs with Herbs and Spices

This type of dish, using very finely minced meat, is popular in North African countries. The delicately spiced meat is fashioned into a thin sausage shape about 10 cm (4 in) long. If your butcher can't mince the lamb for you, do it yourself in a mincer or by chopping it up in small batches in a food processor. Serve with Yoghurt, Tahini and Mint Dip (see page 50).

Makes about 18–20 kebabs

1 kg (2 lb) finely ground lean lamb (or beef or pork)
$\frac{1}{2}$ cup chopped parsley
$\frac{1}{2}$ cup chopped coriander leaves
1 tbsp chopped mint
1 small onion, very finely chopped
1 tsp salt
1 tsp freshly ground black pepper
$\frac{1}{2}$ tsp ground cinnamon
2 tsp ground cumin
$\frac{1}{2}$ tsp ground chilli
1 tsp ground sweet paprika
2 tbsp cold water
2 tbsp olive oil

Place the meat, parsley, coriander, mint, onion, salt, pepper, cinnamon, cumin, chilli, paprika and cold water in a bowl. Mix the ingredients very well by hand until the mixture is like a paste.

Moisten your hands and, using about 2–3 tablespoons of mince, fashion sausage shapes. Push a bamboo stick or metal skewer through the meat and refrigerate the kebabs until you are ready to cook.

Brush the kebabs with oil and cook on a hot barbecue flat plate for a few minutes. Serve immediately.

Spicy Minced Lamb Galette

This is a Middle Eastern-style dish with exotic flavours. Ask your butcher for lean lamb mince. A galette is cooked in the shape of a disc and can be enjoyed with tabouli or a mixed salad.

Serves 4

500 g (1 lb) lean minced lamb
$\frac{1}{4}$ cup cold water
1 tsp tomato paste
1 tsp ground cumin
$\frac{1}{2}$ tsp ground cinnamon
$\frac{1}{2}$ tsp mixed spice
1 tsp chilli paste or $\frac{1}{4}$ tsp chilli powder
3 tbsp finely chopped coriander leaves
salt (optional) and freshly ground black pepper
2 tbsp olive oil

Place the mince, water, tomato paste, cumin, cinnamon, mixed spice, chilli and coriander in a mixing bowl. Season with salt and pepper and combine well. Form into a ball.

Place the ball between two 30 cm (12 in) sheets of baking paper and roll into a galette or disc about 1.5 cm ($\frac{1}{2}$ in) thick.

Heat the oil in a large frying pan. Place the galette carefully in the pan and cook for about 4 minutes. Gently turn the galette over and cook the other side for about 4 minutes.

Cut into four wedges and serve.

Mini-lamb Roast
with Rosemary

Butchers now offer smaller lamb roasts. The best are cuts from
the leg which have the advantage of being lean and tasty, and
ideal for two to four people, depending on the size.

Serves 3

1 red capsicum

1 tbsp olive oil

1 mini-lamb roast, about 400 g (14 oz)

a 10 cm (4 in) sprig of rosemary, broken into small pieces

freshly ground black pepper

10 mushrooms, sliced

$1/2$ cup beef stock

1 tsp cornflour mixed with 1 tbsp water or white wine

salt

Preheat the oven to 180°C (350°F).

Halve the capsicum and remove the seeds. Wash the capsicum
and cut it into bite-sized pieces.

On the stove top, heat the oil in a small flameproof dish or small
roasting tray. Brown the roast all over. Add the capsicum and
rosemary to the tray and season the meat and vegetables with
pepper. Roast the meat in the preheated oven for 20 minutes.
Then transfer the meat to a plate and cover with foil.

Place the roasting tray containing the capsicum on a medium
heat on top of the stove and add the mushrooms. Stir-fry for
2 minutes, then add the stock and bring to the boil. Stir in the
cornflour mixture and boil for 1 minute. Season with a little salt
and pepper.

Slice the lamb very thinly and season with a little salt and pepper.
Serve the lamb on plates with the vegetable sauce.

Lamb and Haricot Bean Ragout

Cook this delicious, hearty ragout in early spring when lamb is excellent and the weather still cool. Remember to start soaking the beans the night before.

Serves 4–6

1 tbsp olive oil

about 1 kg (2 lb) boned, trimmed lamb shoulder, cut into large cubes

1 cup dried haricot beans, soaked in 4 cups water for 12 hours or overnight

1 medium-sized carrot, diced

1 small onion, diced

3 sprigs of lemon thyme, finely chopped

2 cloves garlic, crushed

2 tbsp tomato paste

2 tbsp plain flour

about $\frac{1}{2}$ cup dry white wine

400 g (14 oz) can diced tomato

2 cups beef stock

salt and freshly ground black pepper

3 tbsp chopped parsley

Heat the oil in a large non-stick pot and brown the lamb all over for a few minutes. Transfer the lamb to a bowl.

Add the carrot, onion and lemon thyme to the pan and cook, stirring, for 3 minutes.

Return the meat to the pot, add garlic and tomato paste and stir well. Sprinkle in the flour, stir and cook on a medium heat for 2 minutes. Add the wine, diced tomato and stock and stir well. Add the drained beans, season with salt and pepper and bring to the boil.

Reduce to a simmer, cover with foil tucked down inside the pot and a lid, and cook on low heat for about 2 hours or until the beans and meat are tender.

Stir in the parsley just before serving. Serve with a green salad.

You can replace the dried haricot beans with 2 x 400 g (14 oz) cans of beans. Drain them and add to the dish half an hour before the end of cooking.

New 'Trim Lamb' Shanks

I like to cook this tasty winter dish in a flameproof, cast-iron dish. The new 'trim lamb' shanks have less fat and the end tendons are trimmed in such a way that the meat cooks more easily. Plan ahead as this dish needs to cook for around 2 hours.

Serves 4

2 tbsp olive oil

1 tsp tomato paste

1 tsp ground cumin

1 tsp chilli paste

4 new 'trim lamb' shanks, sometimes called 'frenched' lamb shanks

3 sprigs of thyme

3 tbsp white wine

4 roma tomatoes, cut into small pieces

2 cloves garlic, crushed

salt and freshly ground black pepper

2 tbsp chopped parsley or chopped coriander leaves

Preheat the oven to 150°C (300°F).

In a small bowl, mix half the oil with the tomato paste, cumin and chilli paste. Brush or rub the meat with this paste.

On the stove top, heat the remaining oil in a flameproof casserole dish and brown the meat for a few minutes. Add the thyme, wine, tomato and garlic, and season with a little salt and pepper. Bring to a simmer, cover the dish and cook in the preheated oven for 1 hour.

After that time, turn the meat over, then cook for a further 30 minutes. Then turn the meat again and cook uncovered in the oven for about 30 minutes more or until the meat falls away from the bone.

Just before serving, stir in the chopped parsley and serve with mashed potato and a green salad.

Grilled Pork Cutlet with Mashed Sweet Potato

Choose fresh-looking pork and ask your butcher to trim off as much visible fat as possible.

Serves 2

1 tbsp olive oil

1 tsp dried oregano

1 tsp coriander seeds, crushed

$1/2$ tsp ground sweet paprika

freshly ground black pepper

2 pork cutlets, each about 150 g (5 oz)

2 medium-sized orange-coloured sweet potatoes, about 300 g (10 oz) total

salt

$1/2$ cup milk or skim milk

2 tbsp finely sliced coriander leaves

$1/4$ lemon

On a plate combine the oil, oregano, crushed coriander seeds, paprika and a little pepper. Rub the meat with this preparation and refrigerate if not using immediately.

Peel the sweet potatoes and cut into bite-sized pieces. Place in a saucepan, cover with water, season with salt and bring to the boil. Cook until soft, then drain.

Bring the milk to the boil in a saucepan. Add the cooked sweet potato and mash it. Season to taste with salt and pepper and stir in the coriander.

While the sweet potatoes are cooking, cook the cutlets either on a grill plate, under the grill or in a non-stick frypan for about 4 minutes on each side or until cooked. Season with a little salt.

Place the pork on plates with the sweet potato mash, squeeze some lemon juice over the meat and serve.

Pork Stir-fry with Apricots

Fans of pork meat usually like sweet things and the apricot flavour goes perfectly. Buy the meat already prepared for stir-frying from your supermarket or cut thin, bite-sized strips from a piece of pork sirloin.

Serves 2

250 g (8 oz) plain pork stir-fry

1 tsp cornflour

2 tsp rice wine

2 tbsp soy sauce

about 200 g (7 oz) snow peas

1 tbsp vegetable oil

2 thin slices ginger

$^1/_2$ clove garlic, chopped

8 apricot halves, canned or fresh

3 tbsp water

$^1/_2$ tsp sesame oil

$^1/_2$ tsp chilli paste, optional

Place the pork, cornflour, rice wine and half the soy sauce in a bowl and mix together.

Top and tail the snow peas and place in a medium-sized bowl. Cover with boiling water, then drain after 3 minutes.

Heat the vegetable oil in a wok. Add the ginger, garlic and meat and stir-fry on a high heat until the pork is well browned. Add the apricot halves and the water and cook for 1 minute, while stirring.

Add the snow peas, sesame oil, remaining soy sauce and the chilli paste and stir well to combine. Reheat and serve with rice.

Pork Satays

I use pork sirloin in this dish because of its balance of flavour and tenderness. It is important to marinate the meat for several hours and to avoid drying it out through overcooking. Soak twelve bamboo sticks in cold water for 15 minutes before using them.

Makes 12 satays

10 roasted macadamia nuts
5 cm (2 in) piece of tender lemongrass, finely sliced
2 tbsp soy sauce
1 tsp sugar
2 cloves garlic
2 tsp ground cumin
$\frac{1}{2}$ tsp ground turmeric
2 tsp ground coriander
1 tsp chilli paste
1 tbsp vegetable oil
600 g ($1\frac{1}{4}$ lb) pork sirloin, cut into 1.5 cm ($\frac{1}{2}$ in) cubes
4 lemon or lime wedges
a quantity of peanut sauce (optional, see page 169)

Place the macadamia nuts, lemongrass, soy sauce, sugar, garlic, cumin, turmeric, coriander, chilli paste and oil in a small food processor and blend to a paste.

Toss the pork cubes in this paste, then cover and marinate in the refrigerator for at least 2 hours.

Thread the pork cubes onto twelve satay sticks. Barbecue or grill them on a medium heat for 3–4 minutes on each side.

Serve the satays with lemon or lime wedges and some peanut sauce.

Put Some Spice in Your Life

Learn to recognise spices by their shape, colour, smell and taste. Most spices, for instance cumin, coriander, fennel and nutmeg, are mild, sweet and fruity, with warming overtones. Turmeric and saffron both add an aromatic flavour and yellow colour to a dish. Few spices are hot. The most common hot ones are cayenne and chilli pepper, black pepper and mustard. Curry powders vary in taste, strength, colour and texture, depending on which spices have been used.

Chew or suck unfamiliar spices, (for example, cumin, caraway and cardamom) to understand their flavour and to learn to recognise it. Memorise which spices go well with certain foods, e.g. fennel seeds with fish, cumin with lamb, etc.

Buy ground spices in small quantities only, in sealed packs or jars, and choose them with strong, natural colour. An open pack of ground spice is best used within two months. If you want to grind your own spices, select firm-looking whole spices that are not blemished, discoloured or mouldy. Store opened spices in tightly closed containers away from sunlight.

Once you become more knowledgeable and confident, you'll be able to combine your own favourite mix of spices.

Allspice has the flavours characteristic of several other spices, such as cloves, nutmeg and cinnamon. It's often used in puddings or minced meat preparations, and also with pork and vegetables. Used mostly ground.

Caraway has a warm aromatic flavour. It looks a bit like cumin and has a hint of anise. Caraway seeds are mostly used whole.

Chilli is a very hot spice and needs to be used in moderation. Some chillies have a more aromatic and fruity flavour than others. Avoid giving chilli to young children and the elderly. Can be used dry, powdered or fresh. Fresh chillies are easy to grow in a pot.

Cardamom is one of the most aromatic spices and the smell is really exotic. It's used in many Indian dishes and is one of the spices often used in curry powder. It can also add a magical touch to poached red fruits and plums. The seeds come in pods and are used whole or ground and mixed with other spices.

Cinnamon has a superb warm, aromatic and sensuous perfume and is fabulous in curries and North African casseroles, and desserts, especially those using apples. It is used ground or in sticks.

Cloves are a very strong, sharp spice that goes well in broths and stocks, and on the Christmas ham. It's often used ground in curries or in mixed spice preparations, and can be used ground or whole.

Coriander seeds provide the main spice in curry powder. The whole seeds can be used in Mediterranean dishes, especially with vegetables. They are sometimes crushed a little. Used whole, ground or crushed.

Cumin has a strong, warm aroma and is an important spice in curry powder and in North African and Mediterranean food. I like to sprinkle a few seeds on lamb chops before cooking them. The seeds can be ground or used whole.

Fennel seeds have a distinctive anise flavour, and are superb with barbecued, grilled or baked fish. They can be replaced by celery seeds or aniseed.

Mustard seeds are not only used by Europeans to make mustard, but are also widely used in many Asian and Indian dishes, especially vegetable or vegetarian preparations. There are several varieties. Use them whole or crushed.

Nutmeg is very aromatic and floral, almost exotic. A pinch of grated nutmeg goes a long way in seasoning a white sauce or a dish of spinach or mushrooms.

Paprika is a very popular spice in central Europe. Paprika is sweet with warm, aromatic vegetable flavours and is handy for its red colour. It is used ground.

Pepper is an extremely popular spice with a pungent, almost hot but refreshing taste. Peppercorns are used in most savoury European dishes and are an important element of Indian cuisine. Use whole, ground or crushed. A pepper grinder is a must in any kitchen.

Star anise and **aniseed** both infuse a delicate anise flavour to savoury and sweet dishes. They're best used in moderation. They can be used with curry spices, especially in fish and poultry dishes, and with vanilla when flavouring poached fruits, such as peaches and plums.

Rabbit Casserole with Mushrooms and Herbs

TO JOINT A RABBIT

Using a boning knife or a cleaver, cut through the joints where the front legs connect to the body. Then cut off the back legs in the same way. Cut the body through the backbone into 3 or 4 pieces.

Rabbit meat is tasty and very lean, making it a good source of protein. A wild rabbit may take a bit longer to cook than a farmed one, and you need to cook it in an flameproof casserole dish with a tight-fitting lid.

Serves 4

3 large tomatoes

2 tbsp olive oil

a 1 kg (2 lb) rabbit, jointed

2 sprigs of lemon thyme, chopped

1 tbsp plain flour

$1/2$ cup dry white wine

$1/2$ cup veal stock or a stock cube and water

1 clove garlic, crushed

salt and freshly ground black pepper

about 20 mushrooms

3 tbsp chopped parsley

1 tbsp finely sliced basil or coriander leaves

juice of $1/2$ lemon

Preheat the oven to 180°C (350°F).

Halve the tomatoes, squeeze out the juice and chop the flesh.

On the stove top, heat the oil in a flameproof casserole dish and lightly brown the rabbit pieces. Stir in the thyme and flour, then add the wine. Stir briefly, then add the stock, tomatoes and garlic and season with salt and pepper. Cover with foil and a lid, and bake in the preheated oven for about 1$1/4$ hours or until the rabbit is tender.

Place the dish on top of the stove. Stir in the mushrooms, then simmer, uncovered, until the mushrooms are cooked.

Just before serving, add the parsley, basil and lemon juice.

Spicy Rabbit Ragout

Adapt this dish to your taste, but it is best not to use too much chilli, as it does not suit everyone. You can always serve some chilli sauce separately.

Serves 4

2 tbsp olive oil

1 onion, finely chopped

2 cloves garlic, finely chopped

$\frac{1}{2}$ green chilli, finely sliced

$\frac{1}{2}$ tsp cumin seeds

1 tsp mustard seeds

a 1 kg (2 lb) rabbit, jointed

1 tbsp plain flour

$\frac{1}{2}$ cup dry white wine

400 g (14 oz) can diced tomatoes

1 tsp turmeric

$\frac{1}{4}$ tsp ground cinnamon

salt and freshly ground black pepper

1 tsp ground cumin

juice of $\frac{1}{2}$ lemon

3 tbsp finely sliced coriander leaves

On the stove top, heat the oil in a flameproof casserole dish. Add the onion and garlic and stir for 1 minute. Add the chilli, cumin seeds and mustard seeds. Stir in the rabbit pieces and cook for 3 minutes. Sprinkle in the flour and stir well.

Add the wine and bring to the boil. Add the tomatoes, turmeric and cinnamon and stir well. Season with salt and pepper, cover with foil and a tight-fitting lid and cook in the oven for about $1\frac{1}{2}$ hours, stirring once or twice during the cooking. Cook longer if the rabbit is not done.

Just before serving, stir in the ground cumin, lemon juice and coriander.

DESSERTS & BAKING

Dessert after an everyday meal is not always a necessity, but it can provide variety in our diet. If you don't have a problem with cholesterol, a piece of cheese or some yoghurt or other dairy dessert is delicious as well as a good source of calcium. Fresh fruit is excellent and you can learn to prepare fruit in many ways, such as poaching, baking, or in fruit salads, to mention only a few. Involve your children in preparing special desserts. They really love it and, for them, it may be the beginning of a long love affair with cooking.

Exotic Fruits in Grapefruit Juice

Choose the ripest fruits for this special fruit salad, then you won't need to add sugar or honey to sweeten it. Feel free to create your own version, and if you must make it in advance, make sure the all fruit is covered or coated with the fruit juice. Cover the bowl with plastic wrap and store it in the refrigerator until 10 minutes before serving.

Serves 4

juice of 2 grapefruit

2 passionfruit

2 kiwifruit

1 mango

2 sugar bananas

8 lychees, fresh or canned

Squeeze the grapefruit juice into a bowl. Halve the passionfruit and scoop the pulp into the bowl.

Peel and dice the mango and add it to the bowl. Peel the kiwifruit, cut each into eight pieces and add them to the bowl.

Peel the bananas, cut each into 5 mm ($^1/_4$ in) slices and add them to the bowl. Peel the lychees, remove the stones and add the fruit to the bowl.

Stir the fruit and serve.

Gabriel's Festive
Fruit Salad

Serve this exotic fruit salad in tall parfait coupes with a
scoop of gourmet vanilla ice-cream or home-made ice-cream
(see page 278).

Serves 8

2 oranges

3 tbsp caster sugar

4 passionfruit

2 kiwifruit

2 mangoes

$^1/_2$ pink pawpaw

2 pink grapefruit

30 cherries or 250 g (8 oz) fresh raspberries

15 macadamia nuts, chopped into small pieces

Squeeze the juice of the oranges into a bowl and mix in the sugar.
Halve the passionfruit, scoop out their flesh and add to the bowl.

Peel the kiwifruit and cut them into 5 mm ($^1/_4$ in) slices. Peel
the mangoes and dice the flesh. Using a melon baller, scoop out
balls of pawpaw flesh. Add the kiwifruit, mango and pawpaw
to the bowl.

Using a sharp knife, peel the grapefruit, making sure to remove
all the white pith below the skin. Carefully segment each
grapefruit and add to the bowl.

Pit the cherries and add them to the bowl. Stir in the macadamia
nuts and serve.

Baked Apricots with Raspberries and Almonds

The sweet flavours of summer shine in this colourful dessert. You can replace the apricots with nectarines or peaches, and the raspberries with blueberries, blackberries or pitted cherries.

Serves 4

8–12 ripe apricots

200 g (7 oz) raspberries

1/2 cup apple juice, orange juice or water

2 tbsp brown sugar

4 tbsp flaked almonds

Preheat the oven to 200°C (400°F).

Wash and halve the apricots and remove the stones. Place the apricot halves cut side up in a gratin or oven dish. Dot the spaces in between with raspberries. Pour the juice over the fruit and sprinkle with sugar.

Bake in the preheated oven for 20 minutes or until the apricots are soft.

Lightly brown the almonds in a warm frying pan (take care as they burn quickly!) and sprinkle them over the baked fruit just before serving.

Serve on its own or with yoghurt, cream or ice-cream.

Poached Pears

Serve these pears in a little syrup or drain them and serve with
raspberry sauce, yoghurt, cream or ice-cream. Or serve them in
the French way with some chocolate sauce and vanilla ice-cream
(see page 278).

Serves 4

1 1/2 cups sugar

6 cups water

1/2 vanilla bean

1 small cinnamon stick

rind of 1 orange (use a peeler)

4 pears (Williams, Packham, Beurre Bosc)

In a large saucepan, bring the sugar, water, vanilla, cinnamon
and orange rind to the boil.

Peel the pears neatly, leaving the stalks intact. Remove the end
part of the core using a melon baller.

Add the pears to the simmering syrup and poach for 15–20 minutes
or until tender. The period will depend on the ripeness of the
pears. Leave the pears to cool in the syrup, then refrigerate until
10 minutes before serving.

Natural Yoghurt with Raspberries and Orange

Adjust this easy dessert to suit your taste and the season. Replace the raspberries and orange with strawberries, fresh apricots, peaches, mandarins, pears, etc. You can use low-fat yoghurt if you prefer.

Serves 4

2 cups natural or Greek-style yoghurt

2 tbsp raspberry jam

200 g (7 oz) raspberries

1 large orange

icing sugar (optional)

Whip the yoghurt and raspberry jam for about 30 seconds, then fold in the raspberries.

Using a knife, peel the orange, removing the white pith as well. Slice the orange into eight thin slices.

Place the yoghurt in bowls and top with the orange slices. Dust with icing sugar and serve.

Rhubarb and Apple Compote with Dates and Walnuts

Select medium-sized rhubarb stalks, as the large ones can be stringy. Serve with yoghurt or ice-cream.

Serves about 6

6–8 rhubarb stalks

2 large apples, e.g. Granny Smith, Golden Delicious

4 tbsp caster sugar

$1/2$ vanilla bean, cut in half lengthwise

about $1/3$ cup cold water

3–4 cm ($1^1/2$ in) stick of cinnamon

6–12 fleshy dates

$1/2$ cup walnut halves

Trim the rhubarb of leaves and cut off the base. Wash the stalks and cut them into 5–6 cm (2 in) pieces. Place in a saucepan.

Peel, quarter and core the apples. Cut each quarter in half and add them to the pan.

Sprinkle the sugar over the rhubarb and apple. Add the vanilla and water and cover the pan with a tight-fitting lid. Cook on a medium heat for 10 minutes.

Add the cinnamon stick and dates and cook, covered, for a further 5 minutes.

Remove the cinnamon and add the walnuts. Stir in well and transfer to a bowl to cool.

Salad of Strawberries, Mango, Pineapple and Sugar Banana

Make this fruit salad when strawberries are really sweet-smelling so as to avoid adding too much sugar to the salad. Ask your greengrocer to help you choose a ripe pineapple.

Serves 8

3 punnets strawberries, about 750 g (1 1/2 lb) altogether

2 cups orange juice

1 tbsp sugar (optional if the fruits are very sweet)

1 pineapple

3 sugar bananas

1 large mango or 1/2 papaya

Wash and hull the strawberries and cut into quarters. Place strawberries, orange juice and sugar in a bowl.

Peel the pineapple and cut out the eyes. Slice the pineapple into long quarters. Cut out the core and cut the pineapple into 1 cm (1/2 in) pieces. Add to the bowl and stir gently.

Peel and slice the bananas and add to the bowl. Peel and dice the mango or papaya and add to the bowl.

Serve immediately or cover with plastic film and refrigerate until 10 minutes before serving.

For a more luscious texture, you can blend half the strawberries to a purée then mix them with the orange juice.

Shortcrust Pastry

This easy-to-prepare pastry is handy for fruit pies and flans. The easiest way to make it is in an electric mixer, but you can also use a blender or do it by hand, which is great fun.

Makes 1 pie serving 6–8 or a tart serving 10

1 tbsp caster sugar

1 tsp salt

180 g (6 oz) butter, cut into small dice

1 large egg

2 tbsp milk

250 g (8 oz) plain flour, sifted

Place the sugar, salt and butter in an electric mixer fitted with the beater attachment and beat until almost combined. Add the egg and milk and beat for a few seconds more. Add flour all at once and beat on a low speed until the ingredients are just mixed.

Using your hands, form the pastry into a ball and flatten it slightly. Wrap in plastic film, in foil or in a towel and place in the refrigerator for at least 1 hour to rest before using.

There is nothing better than home-made pastry. Second best is fresh pastry you buy from a friendly baker. Frozen pastry is very convenient but not quite as nice. The tastiest pastries are made with butter.

Apple Pie

A classic family dessert. Make sure to involve your children in this recipe, teaching them how to handle the pastry and slice the apples. You will need a 20–22 cm (8 in) lift-out flan tin.

Serves 8

4 medium Granny Smith or other apples

2 tbsp brown sugar

1/4 tsp cinnamon

3 tsp cornflour

1 quantity shortcrust pastry (see facing page) or 2 sheets frozen
   shortcrust pastry

1 egg yolk mixed with 1 tsp cold water

about 30 g (1 oz) butter, cut into small dice

1/4 lemon

Preheat the oven to 220°C (425°F).

Peel, halve and core the apples, then slice them thinly. Place in a bowl and toss with the sugar, cinnamon and cornflour.

Cut the pastry in two, making one piece twice as large as the other. Roll out the large piece to line the base and sides of the flan tin and prick the base with a fork. Brush the pastry with a little diluted egg yolk and fill the pastry with layers of apple slices. Dot with butter and squeeze lemon juice over the apple.

Roll out the remaining pastry and prick it a few times with a fork. Lay it over the pie, trimming away any excess dough. Pinch the top and sides together to seal the pie and brush the top with the remaining diluted egg yolk. If you wish, use any leftover pastry to make a pattern on top, for example, criss-cross lines, leaves, etc.

Bake the pie in the preheated oven for 10 minutes, then reduce the temperature to 180°C (350°F) and cook for a further 30–35 minutes. When cooked, the base of the pie should be dry and browned.

Lemon and Pear
Rice Pudding

This satisfying and nourishing pudding is as popular with children as it is with adults and makes a great winter dessert.

Serves 4–6

200 g (7 oz) short-grain rice
6 dried pears, soaked in cold water for 2 hours
4 cups milk
3 tbsp caster sugar
1 tbsp finely grated lemon rind
juice of 1 lemon

Place the rice in a saucepan with a large amount of cold water. Bring to the boil and boil for 4 minutes. Drain the rice.

Drain the pears and dice them.

In a large saucepan, bring the milk to the boil. Add the rice, bring to a slow simmer, cover and cook for about 35 minutes, after which time the mixture should be creamy and the rice cooked.

Add the sugar, lemon rind and drained, diced pears. Stir well and cook for a further 2–3 minutes. Stir in the lemon juice and pour into a deep serving dish to set.

The pudding can be eaten warm, but I prefer it cold, after it has set.

Lemon Delicious

With its sharp, sweet lemon flavour, this delicious dessert is half-pudding, half-soufflé. Cook it in a large porcelain or glass mould or in individual soufflé moulds.

Serves 6–8

50 g (1½ oz) soft butter, cut into small dice
1 cup caster sugar
finely grated rind of 2 lemons
4 eggs, separated
⅓ cup self-raising flour, sifted
juice of 3 lemons
1½ cups milk
a pinch of cream of tartar

Preheat oven to 160°C (325°F).

Cream the butter with half the sugar and the lemon rind. (This can be done in a food processor.) Beat in the egg yolks, then mix in the flour, lemon juice and milk.

Beat the egg whites with the cream of tartar until stiff, then beat in the remaining sugar until the mixture is glossy.

Gently fold the lemon preparation into the egg whites and pour into an ovenproof dish.

Stand the dish in a water-bath. Bake in the preheated oven for 45–50 minutes until it is set and lightly browned.

Serve straight away with cream or ice-cream.

Self-saucing Chocolate Pudding

Keep this dessert for a cold weekend when you need a little comfort food.

Serves 6

1 cup self-raising flour

4 tbsp cocoa

60 g (2 oz) butter

$\frac{1}{2}$ cup caster sugar

1 egg, beaten

$\frac{1}{2}$ cup chopped walnuts

$\frac{1}{2}$ cup milk

$\frac{3}{4}$ cup brown sugar

2 cups boiling water

a little icing sugar for dusting

Preheat the oven to 190°C (375°F).

Sift the flour and 2 tablespoons of the cocoa.

Cream the butter and sugar. Add the egg and walnut pieces and mix well. Stir in the flour and cocoa and the milk. Pour the mixture into a 2-litre (4-pint) porcelain or glass baking dish or into a large soufflé dish.

Mix the brown sugar with the remaining cocoa and sprinkle this over the top of the mixture. Pour the boiling water gently over the pudding then bake in the preheated oven for 45 minutes.

Just before serving, dust lightly with icing sugar.

Serve with ice-cream or cream.

Chocolate-flavoured Set Custards

These custards are best cooked in small, porcelain soufflé moulds (about ⅔ cup each). Involve the kids in the preparation. For a different flavour, replace the cocoa with half a vanilla bean or 2 teaspoons of instant coffee.

Makes 8

3 cups milk

8 egg yolks

⅔ cup caster sugar

1 tbsp Dutch cocoa powder (or more if you wish)

boiling water

Preheat the oven to 180°C (350°F).

Bring the milk to the boil in a saucepan.

Beat the egg yolks and sugar in a mixing bowl until they are well combined. Add the hot milk and cocoa and stir in. Strain into a jug or second bowl, then pour the mixture into the moulds. Place the moulds in a baking dish. Pour boiling water into the tray, so that it reaches 1 cm (½ in) below the top of the moulds. Cover the moulds with greaseproof paper or a flat baking sheet.

Bake the custards in the preheated oven for about 25 minutes or until they are just set. Carefully remove the moulds from the water and place on a rack. Cool, then refrigerate for at least 1 hour before serving.

Crème Caramel

Take care when cooking the caramel, which should turn a rich golden colour but must not burn.

You need eight individual porcelain soufflé moulds.

Serves 8

Caramel
200 g (7 oz) caster sugar

4 tbsp water

1 tsp red wine vinegar

Crème
$1/2$ vanilla bean or 2 drops vanilla essence

4 cups milk

200 g (7 oz) caster sugar

6 medium eggs

Preheat the oven to 180°C (350°F).

In a small saucepan combine 200 g (7 oz) of the caster sugar with the water and vinegar. Bring to the boil and cook until it turns golden. To obtain a full caramel flavour, the ideal colour is a rich golden-brown. Full attention must be given at the last moment to not burning the caramel. When the colour is a deep, rich, golden-brown, quickly pour the caramel into the moulds so that it coats the bottom and goes a little way up the sides.

Place the vanilla bean or essence in the milk and bring to the boil.

Meanwhile, using a whisk, combine the remaining caster sugar and eggs well in a bowl. Pour the boiling milk onto the egg and sugar preparation, whisk well and pass through a fine strainer.

Pour the crème preparation into the caramel-coated moulds and place the moulds in a bain-marie or a baking dish one-third filled with warm water. Bake for 30–40 minutes if you are using individual moulds. If you are using one large mould, it will take about 1 hour. Check the cooking by lightly shaking the mould. It should be set and wobble a little. Remove from the oven and allow to cool before placing in the fridge to chill.

To serve, pass a blade around the sides of each mould and unmould each crème and its caramel onto a flat plate.

Runny Custard

Runny custard
or crème anglaise
as we call it in
France, can be
transformed into
a vanilla ice-
cream simply by
churning it in an
ice-cream maker.
It makes one
of the most
delicious ice-
creams.

This custard is delicious served as a sauce with a sponge, chocolate cake, puddings or fresh fruits.

Makes about 3 cups

2 cups milk
$1/3$ vanilla bean or $1/2$ tsp vanilla essence
6 egg yolks
150 g (5 oz) caster sugar

Split the vanilla bean open lengthwise. Heat the milk and the vanilla bean in a medium-sized saucepan.

In a medium-sized bowl and using a hand-held electric beater, beat the egg yolks with the sugar for about 5 minutes or until light and fluffy.

Pour the hot milk onto the egg mixture, whisking rapidly to stop the eggs from scrambling. Return the custard to the pan and stir continuously for a few minutes on a medium heat with a wooden spoon (making a figure 8) until the mixture coats the back of the spoon. The custard must not boil, or the egg yolks will cook and the custard will curdle.

Strain the custard into a mixing bowl and whisk for a few seconds. Allow to cool, then store in the refrigerator covered with plastic wrap.

Sweet Custard

This is a custard to use between pastry and fruit in a tart or for a soufflé preparation. It's called 'crème patissière' (pastry cream) in French and is a basic recipe that can be flavoured with instant coffee, a little cocoa, chopped chocolate or a liqueur.

Makes about 1^1/$_2$ cups

1 cup milk
^{1}/$_3$ vanilla bean or ^{1}/$_2$ tsp pure vanilla essence
2 egg yolks
50 g caster sugar
25 g plain flour, sifted

Split the vanilla bean open lengthwise. Bring the milk and vanilla bean to the boil in a medium-sized saucepan.

Meanwhile, in a bowl, whisk the egg yolks and caster sugar for about 2 minutes or until they are well combined and smooth. Whisk in the flour until just combined.

Pour the hot milk onto the mixture and stir well with a whisk.

Return the preparation to the saucepan and place the pan back on the stove. While whisking constantly on a medium heat, bring the preparation back to a simmer. It will gradually thicken and when it is just boiling and is a thickish consistency, transfer the contents of the pan to the bowl to cool. Whisk for a few more seconds.

Just before serving, remove the vanilla bean. If storing, allow to cool and cover the cream with plastic wrap before refrigerating.

Home-made Vanilla Ice-cream

This recipe does not require an ice-cream maker. It is easy to make but needs to be prepared at least 4 hours before serving in order to set well.

Serves 6

1¼ cups thickened cream
4 large eggs
a pinch of cream of tartar
1 cup icing sugar, sifted
3 drops vanilla essence

Place a 2-litre (4-pint) container in the freezer to chill – this will serve as a mould for the ice-cream.

Whip the cream until stiff, then refrigerate it.

Separate the eggs. Beat the egg whites with the cream of tartar into stiff peaks. Beat the icing sugar into the whites until firm.

Beat the egg yolks with the vanilla essence for 2 minutes. Gently fold in the whites, then fold in the cream. Pour the preparation into the chilled mould, flatten the top and cover with plastic film. Place in the freezer to set.

Hints for Cooking on a Budget

Buy foods in season when they are cheapest.

Visit fresh food markets where prices are competitive.

When buying fish, look at what is fresh and cheap.

For exciting seasonings, grow herbs in your garden or in pots on the verandah.

Use oil and fat in moderation and use non-stick pans.

Buy groceries in bulk, but don't be overzealous. Check the use-by date.

Learn to cook new dishes of pasta, noodles, rice and potatoes.

Learn to prepare legumes, like beans, lentils and chickpeas.

Cook more vegetables and a little less meat.

Commit yourself to becoming a better cook by learning new dishes.

Soups in winter are filling and nourishing.

Buy wholemeal bread – it's more filling.

Use leftovers the next day – don't wait; they may end up in the bin!

Keep leftovers well covered with plastic film in the fridge.

Discover the beautiful flavours of cheaper cuts of meat, and make stews and casseroles. Make extra and freeze it for another day.

Eat at regular times to avoid snacking.

Buy meat and fish according to weight rather than per slice, for example, buy 600 g (1 1/4 lb) chicken fillets for four people rather than four chicken fillets, which may weigh 800 g (1 1/2 lb) altogether.

Eggs (if you have no problems with cholesterol) are one of the easiest and cheapest snacks.

Blueberry Muffins

The secret of a good muffin is to mix the ingredients rapidly without overmixing, and then to cook the mixture without delay. You can replace the blueberries with raspberries, blackberries, diced apple or diced pear. If you wish, you can replace the plain flours and baking powder with the same quantity of white and wholemeal self-raising flour.

Makes about 12 muffins

melted butter, margarine or vegetable oil to grease the tray
1/2 cup caster sugar
1 tbsp finely grated lemon zest
80 g (3 oz) melted butter, cooled
1 cup milk or 1 cup buttermilk
2 small eggs
1 cup plain wholemeal flour
1 1/2 cups plain white flour
1 tbsp baking powder
250 g (8 oz) blueberries

Preheat the oven to 200°C (400°F).

Brush the muffin tray with a little melted butter.

In a bowl, combine the sugar, lemon zest, melted butter, milk and eggs.

Sift the two types of flour and the baking powder into a large bowl. Pour the blueberries and the milk preparation onto the flour and stir with a wooden spoon until just combined. It's important not to take too long or to overmix. Spoon the preparation immediately into the muffin tray and bake in the preheated oven for 15–20 minutes. When the muffins are cooked, wait 5 minutes then turn them out onto a wire rack to cool.

Pikelets

A real family treat for the colder months. Teach your children or grandchildren to make them – it will increase their confidence in the kitchen.

Makes about 12

1 egg, lightly beaten

1 cup milk

1¼ cups self-raising flour

about 30 g (1 oz) butter or margarine or oil

Combine the egg and milk in a bowl.

Place the flour in a mixing bowl and make a well in the centre of the flour. Pour the milk and egg preparation into the well and whisk to form a smooth batter.

Melt some of the butter in a non-stick frying pan on a medium heat. Place tablespoons of the batter into the pan, and when bubbles appear on the surface of each pikelet, turn it and cook the second side. Remove the pikelets and allow to cool.

Repeat with the remaining batter. Spread the pikelets with a topping of your choice and serve.

Baking Powder

Commercial baking powder is made up of bicarbonate of soda, a mixture of phosphate and some food starch. When this powder is added to a moist preparation and heated, it gives off bubbles (carbon dioxide) and this aerates and lightens the preparation, making it rise. You can make your own mixture equivalent to 1 teaspoon of commercial baking powder by mixing ¼ tsp of bicarbonate of soda with ½ tsp of cream of tartar. This mixture must be used immediately.

Date and Apricot Loaf

In this delicious loaf, which has no added fat or sugar, the moisture is created by puréeing a banana with some soaked apricots. The dried fruits provide sweetness, making it a good snack for the school lunch box.

Makes about 12 slices

25 dried apricots
1 cup cold water
1 banana
1 cup almond meal
3 large eggs
$1/2$ cup self-raising flour
$1/2$ cup sultanas
12 large Californian dates, pitted

Grease a 20 cm (8 in) loaf tin and line the base with baking paper.

Place the apricots in a saucepan with the water. Bring to a simmer, cover and cook for 3 minutes. Remove 15 of the apricots and set aside. Blend the remaining 10 to a purée with the cooking liquid and the banana. Transfer to a large mixing bowl.

Preheat the oven to 180°C (350°F).

Mix the almond meal into the fruit purée, then beat in the eggs. Stir in the flour until it is just mixed. Stir in the remaining whole apricots, the sultanas and the pitted dates.

Pour the mixture into the prepared tin and bake in the preheated oven for about 45 minutes.

Allow to cool for 15 minutes, then pass a thin blade around the edges of the tin and carefully unmould the cake onto a rack.

Serve the cake when it is cold, cutting it into 1.5 cm ($1/2$ in) slices. Store wrapped in foil or in a biscuit tin.

Shortbread Biscuits

These biscuits are easy to make and much appreciated by adults.
Cut the biscuits into the shape you wish, using either a biscuit
cutter or knife. Popular shapes include rectangles, hearts,
Christmas trees and stars.

Makes about 40 biscuits

250 g (8 oz) butter, cut into small cubes and slightly softened
1 tsp finely grated lemon zest
100 g (3$\frac{1}{2}$ oz) icing sugar
330 g (11 oz) plain flour, sifted

Preheat oven to 150°C (300°F).

Place butter, lemon zest and icing sugar in a mixing bowl and
beat, using an electric beater, until well combined. Add sifted
flour then combine until it forms a mass, but don't overmix.
Form this dough into a ball, flatten slightly, then wrap in plastic
film and refrigerate for about 1 hour.

For easier handling, roll out the dough on a sheet of baking
paper. Roll it to a rectangle whose smaller side measures about
18–20 cm (7–8 in) and to a thickness of about 6 mm ($\frac{1}{4}$ in).
Cut the biscuits into 1.5 x 6 cm ($\frac{1}{2}$ x 2 in) rectangles.

Place biscuits on a large oven tray lined with baking paper and
prick each one at least three times with a fork. Bake the biscuits
in the preheated oven for about 25 minutes until they are cooked
and dry underneath.

Cool on a rack then store in an airtight container.

Chocolate Chip and Almond Biscuits

Home-made biscuits are always popular and they taste so much fresher. If you have children, get them involved in the preparation.

Makes approximately 35 biscuits

125 g (4 oz) butter
$1/2$ cup caster sugar
$1/2$ cup brown sugar
1 egg
$1/2$ tsp vanilla essence
$13/4$ cups self-raising flour
pinch of salt
$1/2$ cup Choc Bits
$1/4$ cup slivered almonds

Preheat oven to 180°C (350°F).

Cut butter into small cubes. Place the butter, caster sugar and brown sugar in a large bowl. Using an electric beater, beat the mixture until creamy.

Crack the egg into a small bowl and lightly beat with a fork. Add beaten egg and vanilla essence to the creamed butter and sugar and stir.

Place the flour and salt in the sifter and sift over the mixture. Add choc bits and slivered almonds and mix well.

Shape the mixture into small balls about the size of a walnut, and place on an oven tray about 6 cm (2 in) apart.

Bake in preheated oven for 10–12 minutes or until golden brown. Remove biscuits with a lifter and allow to cool on a rack. Once cool, store in an airtight container.

Macadamia Crescents

This is one of my favourite biscuits to enjoy with a cup of tea or coffee. They are very easy to make. You can replace the macadamia nuts with blanched almonds or skinned hazelnuts.

Makes at least 35 biscuits

1/3 cup caster sugar

200 g (7 oz) unsalted butter, cut into pieces

1/2 tsp vanilla essence

a pinch of salt

2 egg yolks

1/3 cup almond meal

2 cups plain flour

3/4 cup raw macadamia nuts, each cut into 3 or 4 pieces

about 100 g (3 1/2 oz) icing sugar for dusting

Preheat the oven to 160°C (325°F).

Place the sugar and butter in an electric mixer fitted with the beater attachment and beat until combined. Add the vanilla, salt, egg yolks and almond meal and beat well. Add the flour and beat until just combined. Transfer the dough to a bowl and mix in the pieces of macadamia nut.

Roll walnut-sized pieces of the dough into 5 cm (2 in) lengths then shape them roughly into crescents.

Grease an oven tray lightly or cover with baking paper. Place the crescents on the tray and bake in the preheated oven for about 15 minutes or until they are light brown. Check the cooking by breaking a biscuit in half to see if it is cooked in the centre.

Cool the biscuits for about 5 minutes before rolling them in icing sugar. Once cold, the biscuits can be stored in an airtight container.

Butter Cake with Passionfruit Icing

This is a great recipe for all family cooks to know. You need a 23 cm (9 in) round or ring cake tin or a 20 cm (8 in) square tin.

Serves 8–12

butter and flour for the cake tin

180 g (6 oz) sugar

3 large eggs

2 tsp finely grated lemon zest

180 g (6 oz) butter, just melted

pulp of 1 passionfruit (optional)

90 g (3 oz) plain flour

90 g (3 oz) self-raising flour

Preheat oven to 180°C (350°F).

Grease the cake tin with butter and dust with flour.

Beat sugar, eggs and lemon zest for a few minutes until light and creamy. Mix in melted butter and passionfruit pulp. Sift both types of flour over the top and fold in until just mixed. Don't overwork it.

Pour the mixture into the prepared tin and bake in the preheated oven for about 35–40 minutes. A skewer inserted should come out clean.

Allow to cool in the tin for about 5 minutes before turning the cake out onto a cake rack. Allow the cake to cool before icing with the Passionfruit Icing on page 291. Let the icing set before serving.

You can cut the cake in half horizontally and spread a little whipped cream or jam in between the halves. The top can be iced with a flavour of your choice then decorated with fresh fruits, such as strawberries or raspberries, or with Smarties or other lollies.

Sponge Cake

If you wish to make a chocolate sponge, reduce the quantity of flour to 220 g (7$\frac{1}{2}$ oz) and sift the flour with 2 tablespoons of cocoa.

This is an excellent base for a birthday cake, and it looks lovely decorated with icing and garnished with whipped cream and fruits, such as strawberries. You need a 25 cm (11 in) cake tin, buttered and floured, or two tins of 20-cm (8-in) diameter.

Serves 12–14

8 eggs
250 g (8 oz) caster sugar
250 g (8 oz) plain flour, sifted
100 g (3$\frac{1}{2}$ oz) unsalted butter, just melted

Preheat oven to 180°C (350°F).

Break the eggs into a large bowl. Add sugar and, using an electric beater, beat until the mixture forms a thick ribbon. This takes about 10 minutes. To incorporate as much air as possible, make large movements with the beater.

Add the sifted flour all at once and, using a rubber spatula, fold it in gently but quickly. When you see that the last of the flour has disappeared, incorporate the melted butter quickly but gently.

Pour the mixture into the prepared tin and smooth the top with a spatula. Bake in the preheated oven for 35–40 minutes for a large cake or about 30 minutes for the smaller ones. Test the cooking by pressing lightly in the centre. If the sponge springs back, it is done.

When the sponge is cooked, remove from the oven and leave to cool for a few minutes before gently unmoulding onto a cooling rack.

Poppyseed Cake
with Lemon Icing

This cake is a favourite for afternoon tea and is lovely made in a kugelhopf or ring mould.

Serves 8–10

125 g (4 oz) butter, softened but not melted

finely grated rind of 1 lemon

1 tbsp orange blossom or other honey

1¼ cups caster sugar

1 egg yolk

1 cup milk

300 g (10 oz) plain flour, sifted

a pinch of salt

2 tsp baking powder

4 tbsp poppyseeds

4 egg whites

Preheat the oven to 160°C (325°F).

In a large mixing bowl, cream the softened butter, lemon rind, honey and 1 cup of the sugar until smooth. Mix in the egg yolk and milk. Stir in the flour, salt, baking powder and poppy seeds.

Beat the egg whites until stiff peaks form. Add the remaining ¼ cup sugar and beat a little more. Fold the beaten egg whites into the mixture, then pour it into a greased ring tin and bake for about 40 minutes.

Remove the cake from the oven and allow it to cool for about 5 minutes before unmoulding it onto a wire rack.

When the cake is cold, spread it with the Lemon Icing on page 291, using the blade of a knife or a small spatula.

Chocolate Cake

Just a small slice of this dense chocolate cake will satisfy most appetites.

Serves 8–12

200 g (7 oz) dark cooking chocolate, as bitter as possible

3 eggs, separated

100 g (3$\frac{1}{2}$ oz) caster sugar

60 g (2 oz) unsalted butter, cut into small pieces

100 g (3$\frac{1}{2}$ oz) walnuts, chopped

80 g (3 oz) plain flour, sifted

60 g (2 oz) sultanas

2 tbsp brandy, Drambuie or rum (optional)

a pinch of cream of tartar

Butter and flour a 20 cm (8 in) cake tin. Preheat the oven to 200°C (400°F).

Break the chocolate into pieces and melt, either in a large bowl over a saucepan of hot water or in the microwave.

In a second bowl, beat the egg yolks and sugar until fluffy and white.

Incorporate the butter into the melted chocolate mixture (away from the heat).

Add the egg yolk preparation to the chocolate mixture, then gently mix in the walnuts, flour, sultanas and brandy.

Add the cream of tartar to the egg whites then beat until stiff. Using a metal spoon, fold the beaten whites into the cake mixture, then pour the mixture into the prepared cake tin.

Cook in the preheated oven for 30 minutes – the cake must remain quite moist in the centre.

Remove from the oven, wait 10 minutes, then carefully turn the cake out onto a wire rack. Allow to cool before icing with the Chocolate Icing on page 291 then refrigerate for 1 hour before serving.

Passionfruit Icing

about 1 cup icing sugar
pulp of about 2 passionfruit

Sift icing sugar into a bowl. Slowly add some of the passionfruit pulp until
the icing sugar is moist but still thickish. You may not use all the
passionfruit. If the icing is too thin, add a little extra icing sugar.

Lemon Icing

1 tsp butter, softened but not melted
$1^1/_2$ cups pure icing sugar, sifted
1 tsp finely grated lemon rind
juice of 1 lemon

Place the softened butter in a bowl. Add the lemon rind and icing sugar.
Gradually whisk in the lemon juice until you have a spreadable icing. You
may not use all the lemon juice. If the icing is too dry, add a little cold water
a teaspoon at a time.

Chocolate Icing

2 tbsp cream
100 g ($3^1/_2$ oz) semi-sweet dark chocolate
$^1/_4$ tsp instant coffee (optional)

Bring the cream to the boil in a small saucepan. Remove from heat and stir in
the chocolate until it is melted and the mixture is smooth. Stir in the coffee.
Pour the icing over the cake and spread thinly.

Conversions

Both metric and imperial quantities are given. Use either all metric or all imperial, as the two are not necessarily interchangeable. The following standard metric measurements have been used:

1 teaspoon = 5 millilitres or 0.1691 fluid ounces

1 tablespoon = 15 millilitres or 0.5072 fluid ounces

1 cup = 250 millilitres or 8.454 fluid ounces

Acknowledgements

As with all of my cookbooks I am most grateful to my wife, Angie, who took part in almost all aspects of this project. Thanks also to many home cooks and friends who have helped me in my research.

Thanks to Paul Davey, Alison Hodge and Paul Ireland from the Cancer Council of Victoria; to Jackie Cooper from the Heart Foundation; to Karen Inge and Christine Roberts for their advice on nutrition; and to Professor Louise Bearley Messer for her advice on how to take care of our teeth.

Special thanks to my greengrocer, Toscano of Kew, and my fishmonger, Claringbolds, at the Prahran Market.

As always thanks go to my publishers, Allen & Unwin, especially Sue Hines and Rachel Lawson; to designer Nick Mau, photographer Adrian Lander and food stylist Kyle Barnett.

INDEX